conception and and childbirth

His (Christ's) Way

LaShela Annette Jones

authorHOUSE®

AuthorHouse™
1663 Liberty Drive
Bloomington, IN 47403
www.authorhouse.com
Phone: 1 (800) 839-8640

Published by AuthorHouse 12/03/2018

ISBN: 978-1-5462-5965-7 (sc)
ISBN: 978-1-5462-5966-4 (hc)
ISBN: 978-1-5462-5967-1 (e)

Library of Congress Control Number: 2018910790

Print information available on the last page.

This book is printed on acid-free paper.

Elect-Lady LaShela Annette Jones

The elder unto the elect lady and her children, whom I love in the truth; and not I only, but also all they that have known the truth; For the truth's sake, which dwelleth in us, and shall be with us forever.

II John 1:1-2

DEDICATION

This book is dedicated to Jesus Christ. He inspired me to write this book. I know it was Him working through me to bring His will on earth as it is in Heaven. To my husband, Pastor Barry Jones Sr., I truly thank God for you. Oh, how I praise God that you are perfect for me. I was truly blessed to be found by you. Never could I have chosen rightly for myself a loving soulmate like you. I dedicate this book to my eleven children Delvin, Barry, Zachery, Hannah, Marion, Temperance, Nathan, Nahum, Naomi, Phebe, and Miracle. Wow, how was I handpicked to raise such a beautiful family? I thank God for all of you, you all bring such a blessing to my life, with each passing day. Lastly, I dedicate this book to all babies who have been and will be hindered by contraceptives, and those babies who have died and will die by way of abortions.

TABLE OF CONTENTS

FOREWORD BY PASTOR BARRY JONES, SR.

We live in a generation that has been desensitized to the truth. The truth has become what we believe or accept, instead of what is fact. Society has accepted Satan's corrupt plan to steal, to kill and to destroy our future by destroying our seed. If Satan kills our seed, then he has successfully weakened or destroyed the next generations of Christians.

Elect Lady LaShela Jones has decided to confront the societal norms head on with a refreshing dose of the truth. She is a Holy Ghost filled Minister of the Gospel of Christ, with many remarkable testimonies during the delivery process of our eleven children. Tears of joy, pain and sorrow has been the legacy of this beautiful mother. Many, intellectuals have decided to reject the truth regarding childbirth and contraceptive use.

However; people of God, there will be a Day of Judgment. The societal norms man's opinions, and worldly wisdom will come face to face with the truth. Until then, please allow Elect Lady Jones the opportunity to share with you some of her testimonies as you read the following pages. Please pray that Jesus Christ opens your heart to understand and accept the truth as you read this book. John 8:31 says, *"And ye shall Know the truth, and the truth shall make you free."* Please know that, the purpose of this book is not to bring condemnation, but education and reconciliation. Elect-Lady LaShela Jones is the passionate voice of the unborn victims of birth control.

Pastor Barry Jones Sr.
Manna Ministries Inc.
Mobile, Alabama

FOREWORD BY PASTOR
DEREK S. GANDY

In the face of the written, unadulterated truth of God, people who profess to be "of Christ," and who so emphatically stress their love for Him, prove to be the most egregious offenders against Him and His Word. Today's church people more often rehearse the thoughts and opinions of man more than they do the Word of God. "I think," "I feel," "The way I see it," "In my opinion," and similar sentiments are far too commonplace. There seems to be very little commitment to obeying and sharing what God's Word says. This truth is addressed by Jesus in Matthew 7:21-23. In this book it is refreshing to read the bold Bible exclamations shared by Lady Jay, as she courageously confronts the genocidal spirit the devil has cast on the world; the spirit of abortion, of murder.

This is a topic that is hardly addressed in churches today. Sadly, when explored, it is often flavored with worldly influences. Common sense appears to be the reigning influence in many Christian circles, minimalizing and dismissing instruction from God. The church at large has become so wise until preachers attempt to teach God the beginning and the definition of life. These definitions include condoning abortion, promoting birth control and turning a blind eye to homosexuality. Lady Jay effectively addresses this murderous church of today, which is attempting to package and to sell itself as the Church of God. The real challenge in this reading experience is for the reader to pursue these pages with an open mind and a hungry spirit.

Societal norms, church teachings and religious dogma concerning childbirth are all shown to be great obstacles in keeping folks from receiving this truth. However, Lady Jay effectively explores and shares the true intent of God, which is life. She shares the Godly, Bible verifiable perspective that birth control and abortion are murder. This writing is a good place to begin as churches and parents address these issues with the youth.

Teaching our youth to really appreciate life may result in heightened expectations and a greater sense of responsibility in their own lives. Lady Jay has made this book available for the benefit of all who will hear. Let us begin the conversation, now. Can you hear what The Spirit (The Holy Ghost) is saying to you? As I read this book my thought was and remains, "Jesus' name be praised!"

Pastor Derek Scott Gandy
True Cornerstone Church of the Apostolic Faith, Inc.
Mobile, Alabama

ACKNOWLEDGMENTS

I would like to thank my Savior, Jesus Christ for life, health and strength. I thank Him for saving my soul and filling me with the Holy Ghost. I thank God for water baptism in His name. By His grace I am continuing steadfastly in the apostles' doctrine.

To my husband, Pastor Barry Jones Sr., you are a gift from God. Thank you for all that you do. Thank you for being such a wonderful father to our children. I thank you for the excitement you expressed each time you learned I was expecting. You make being fruitful and multiplying joyful. I will multiply again and again for you. Your love for me is certainly worth it.

To Felicia Myles, thank you for all you've done. To Michelle Brun, thank you for the hours you spent listening to me read this book repeatedly. To Minister Shalanda Glover and Minister Tamiko Henry thank you for checking your emails and giving me positive feedback. Prophetess Marion Collins, thank you for listening to me read. To Sister Shanika Jackson, thank you for expressing your excitement about my book.

To Pastor Derek Scott Gandy, thank you so much. No amount of words can express my appreciation for you helping to edit my book. Nobody but Pastor G says "Lady Jay, you tripping!" It's good to know you still have friends that love you even when you're tripping. You know I'm cracking up, right? I love you, Lady Gandy and G-5.

To Breanna Loyd, thank you for helping me type and type and type. I love you so much. Thank you for listening to me read my book and giving me feedback. To my English professor, Dr. Roxanne Odom, thank you for taking the time to read my book. Your words of encouragement will abide in my heart as I lunge forward in my writing endeavors. I want to acknowledge one of the most sprit filled and spirit led bodies of Christ in Mobile, Alabama, Manna Ministries.

I truly love you all, thank you for following Pastor Jones and me as we follow Christ. I want my mother, Delores Westry, my siblings, Helen, Melvin, Pernita and Alvin to know that I love you all. Thanks to everyone who have contributed to the process of this vision that I have written and made plain. Last but not least, to my babies, Delvin, Barry, Zachery, Hannah, Marion, Temperance, Nathan, Nahum, Naomi, Phebe, and Miracle, I am so honored to be your mother. Thank you for growing with me in God. Thank you for sharing your mom is so many ways. When I look at each of you I know for a fact that being fruitful is right. You are my rewards.

TEACHERS OF
GOOD THINGS

If a sickness of some kind comes upon us, we will take medication or undergo surgery to get our body to function properly. We often look to man to restore God's original functioning of the body, so not to be disabled. Yet, we will submit a normal functioning womb to be medically or surgically disabled. Wow!

Lady J

Teachers of Good Things

"Praise the Lord Sister. How many children y'all have now?" "Nine," I replied. "Is that it," she asked. "If He says so," I replied, pointing towards Heaven. She chanted pitifully, "I hope that's it. I hope that's it." Believe it or not, that was a very short conversation I had with an elder woman at church. I must say my thoughts were, "Why are you hoping that's it? What if I am pregnant right now? If I am pregnant should the child not be here?"

I am not trying to over analyze the situation. "How many children do y'all have now," is a clear indication that my husband and I were viewed as the couple that has all those babies. Come on now, it is clear to see that we have been the topic of discussion at least once. That conversation was wrong on so many levels. The Woman of God's statement would be perfectly okay if it came from an unbeliever. Many Christians view conception and childbirth as only a natural occurrence. There is a spiritual side that we should be aware of as well.

Carnality blinds the eyes of the people of God causing us sometimes to call evil good, and good evil. Let us view that conversation through the eyes of scripture.

3 "The aged women likewise, that they be in behavior as becometh holiness, not false accusers, not given to much wine, teachers of good things;

4 That they may teach the young women to be sober, to love their husbands, to love their children,

5 To be discreet, chaste, keepers at home, good, obedient to their own husbands, that the word of God be not blasphemed."

{Titus 2:3-5} (KJV)

Should married women be taught to love their children, or taught to be sure not to have so many? Elder women should teach the younger women to love their children, not question those who are bearing children in marriage.

The Bible explains that a little leaven, leavens the whole lump. Luke chapter twelve, verses one through seven has an interesting teaching from Jesus. He warns His disciples to beware of the leaven or teachings of the Pharisees.

Jesus called their teaching hypocrisy. Jesus explained, "That nothing will be covered or hid that shall not be known." He compels His disciples, calling them friends and saying, "Be not afraid of them that kill the body and after that can do no more." But rather, He says, "I will forewarn you whom ye shall fear: Fear Him which after he hath killed hath power to cast into hell; yea, I say unto you, fear Him." {Luke 12:5}

In my opinion, it is hypocrisy to profess to serve God, yet justify not allowing the fruit of the body to come forth. Can we all agree that the womb is not controlled by man? Only God can allow offspring to come forth. Unless, of course, we usurp authority over it! Usurp in this context is referring to seizing or to hold (position, office, power, etc.) by force or without legal right. Usurp also means to use without authority or right; it also means to employ wrongfully. Furthermore, to commit forcible or illegal seizure of an office, power, etc. When you usurp power, you put yourself in a position above God. Furthermore, He alone is omnipotent.

He had plans for our children long before our existence. Have faith in God. He has thoughts of peace concerning your family, not evil. *"For I know the thoughts that I think toward you saith the Lord, thoughts of peace, and not of evil, to give you an expected end."* {*Jeremiah 29:11*} Sometimes we do not fear God in areas that we should. Look at an account from the Bible that illustrates reverence and the fear of God.

{Exodus 1:15-17}

15. And the king of Egypt spake to the Hebrew midwives, of which the name of the one was Shiphrah, and the name of the other Puah:

16. And he said, when ye do the office of a midwife to the Hebrew women and see them upon the stools; if it be a son, then ye shall kill him: but if it be a daughter, then she shall live.

17. But the midwives feared God and did not as the king of Egypt commanded them but saved the men children alive."

The children of Israel were fruitful. The Bible says, they increased abundantly and multiplied exceedingly. The king wanted to stop the male children from coming forth. He felt they were mightier than his crew.

He also feared that they would continue to multiply and side with his enemies against him. Poor thing, he placed hard burdens upon Israel, but the more he afflicted them the more they multiplied and grew. The midwives feared God. They knew it was God's will for children to come forth. The king and prince of this world (Satan) have put out a similar decree. He is using midwives, doctors and even **The Church** to discourage fruitfulness. History has a way of repeating itself. I am reminded of King Herod during the time of the birth of Christ. Isaiah's prophecy had finally become reality.

21 And she shall bring forth a son, and thou shalt call his name JESUS: for he shall save his people from their sins.

22 Now all this was done, that it might be fulfilled which was spoken of the Lord by the prophet, saying,

23 Behold, a virgin shall be with child, and shall bring forth a son, and they shall call his name Emmanuel, which being interpreted is, God with us.

24 Then Joseph being raised from sleep did as the angel of the Lord had bidden him and took unto him his wife:

25 And knew her not till she had brought forth her firstborn son: and he called his name JESUS.

{Matthew 1:21-25}

Finally, Jesus was born in Bethlehem of Judaea. The wise men said, "Where is he that is born King of the Jews?" When Herod heard the sayings, he was troubled, and all Jerusalem with him. He tried to get the wise men to collaborate with him, on his plot against Jesus. Thank God the wise men knew right from wrong, and were sensitive to his motives. However, when King Herod learned that the wise men did not honor his request he was angry. He sent forth to kill every child two years old and younger. Herod's plotting did not stop our Savior's life. Once Herod was dead, an angel warned Joseph in a dream that the coast was clear. The angel said, "For they are dead which sought the young child's life."

{Matthew 2:16-20}

16 Then Herod, when he saw that he was mocked of the wise men, was exceeding wroth, and sent forth, and slew all the children that were in Bethlehem, and in all the coasts thereof, from two years old and under, according to the time which he had diligently *inquired of the wise men.*

17 Then was fulfilled that which was spoken by Jeremiah the prophet, saying,

18 In Rama was there a voice heard, lamentation, and weeping, and great mourning, Rachel weeping for her children, and would not be comforted, because they are not.

19 But when Herod was dead, behold, an angel of the Lord appeareth in a dream to Joseph in Egypt,

20 Saying, Arise, and take the young child and his mother, and go into the land of Israel: for they are dead which sought the young child's life.

God is looking for some wise men and women to be sensitive to the plot of the enemy. The wise men of the Bible knew that Herod's plot was to end life. Are there any wise men and women who will take a stand for life today? **The Church** should take on the mentality of the midwives and wise men of the Bible, and let the Lord have his way. Let's get back to fearing God as we should. "For this is the whole duty of man to fear God and keep his commandments."

{Ecclesiastes 12:13}

"Be fruitful and multiply is really a commandment, right," asked Sister Brun? She continues, "He did not say if you want to, or feel up to it be fruitful and multiply." My husband explains it like this; "We place so much emphasis on this life. We fear what may possibly take us out of the earth realm or put us in a position where we cannot function as we desire." That is so true. We expect God to keep our bodies from hurt, harm and danger.

For instance, **if a sickness of some kind comes upon us, we will take medication, undergo surgery, or do whatever it takes to get our body to function as it was created to function.**

However, when it comes to the womb, we will take medication and even undergo surgery to stop our body from functioning as God created it to function. **Whoa!** Think about it! If your head is hurting, will you take an aspirin to get your head to function properly? If you had a heart condition, would you get the necessary treatment to restore <u>normal</u> function? If you had lung problems, would you allow treatment to restore <u>normal</u> function? I 'm sure your response is, "Of course," and my answer would be the same. How can we place greater faith in doctors and in medicine than in our Creator? We often look to man to restore God's **original** functioning of the body, so <u>**not**</u> to be **disable.**

Yet, we will submit a normal functioning womb <u>**to be**</u> medically or surgically **disabled.** <u>**Double Whoa**</u>! Okay, the jury is out. You be the judge. Is this hypocrisy? I am not speaking negatively against medical interventions that are necessary. However, I am certainly speaking against intentionally controlling birth, simply because you do not want children or any more children. I don't want to be labeled as one who kills the body, by what my dear husband calls, "high class genocide." Dictionary.com defines genocide as "the deliberate, systematic, and methodical extermination of a national, racial, political or cultural group."

Speaking of killing the body, I know a young girl who had a child and became pregnant again immediately afterwards. She was told by a friend to keep her baby. However, her family told her to have an abortion. She did have the abortion, but carried guilt and shame for many years. She explained that she received a release after going to a Christian skit one night. The title of the skit was, "Where Will You Spend Eternity? In the play, there was a young lady who was very angry. Her anger caused her one problem after the next. She ended up confessing to a Christian that she had an abortion many years back.

She was angry inside about it. For years she had been affected spiritually, mentally, emotionally, and physically. To make a long story short, she gave her life to Christ then she died. The skit showed her entering heaven and being greeted by her daughter who she aborted. Her child was thirteen. Ironically, that would have been the age of the young girl's child.

The young girl said, she cried hysterically at the skit for two reasons. The first reason was the reality of killing her baby. Secondly, she cried tears of joy, knowing she was forgiven. Likewise, if your heart is pricking you today concerning this topic, right now is a perfect time to ask for forgiveness. Let God come in and give you the release you so desperately deserve. Abortion and many other methods are being used to induce Planned Parenthood today. Where did this teaching of controlled birth come from anyway?

WHERE IT ALL BEGIN

Wow, so it looks like even speaking openly about contraceptives was illegal. Oh my, how far have we fallen to go from speaking about controlled birth being illegal to it being the norm, even in the Body of Christ? How did we become so free to the point of supporting birth control in the house of the Lord?

Lady J

Where it All Began

The person mainly responsible for the birth control movement in the United States was Margaret Sanger. Margaret Higgins Sanger (September 14, 1879 - September 6, 1966) was an American birth control activist, sex educator, and nurse. Sanger popularized the term birth control, opened the first birth control clinic in the U.S., and established organizations that evolved into the Planned Parenthood Federation of America.

I noticed that a birth control activist died the year my husband was born. He was the tenth child of the late **Louella Jones**. Oh, how I praise God that his mother was fruitful and continued to multiply after having nine babies already. She also had two still born years before his conception. Yes, that would have been eleven children prior to my wonderful husband's birth. Praise God she multiplied once more and had a baby girl after him. What a brave woman!

I regret not meeting her and having her to be a part of our children's lives. Sanger's teachings had been around for years at the time of my husband's birth. However, God still had some who were not interested in it. There were women who still chose life over anything that could be obtained in life. Margaret Sanger felt that in order for women to have a "more equal footing" in society and to lead healthier lives, they needed to be able to determine when to bear children.

Here are some more quotes from her book: **The Case of Birth Control**. "For centuries, woman has gone forth with man to till the fields, to feed and clothe the nations. She has sacrificed her life to populate the earth. She has over done her labors. She now steps forth and demands that women shall cease producing in ignorance. To do this she must have knowledge to control birth. This is the first immediate step she must take toward her goal of her freedom."

Sanger's feelings are contrary to the teachings in the Bible, which tells women to be discreet chaste keepers at home. We must remember we were created to be a help meet, not to have "an equal footing." *"I will therefore that the younger women marry, bear children, guide the house, give none occasion to the adversary to speak reproachfully."* {1Timothy 5:14}

Look at more teachings from Sanger. "I ask you which is more moral to urge women to have only those children she desires and can care for, or to delude her into breeding thoughtlessly, which is America's definition of morality? "She continued, "You will agree with me that a woman should be free. Yet no adult woman who is ignorant of the means to <u>prevent</u> <u>conception</u> can call herself free. No woman can call herself free who cannot choose the time to be a mother or not as she sees fit. This should be woman's first demand," she exclaimed.

A woman should not choose the time to be a mother when she sees fit, because that power belongs to God. If a woman is not ready to be a mother when God sees fit, she should remain in celibacy. Sanger's theory that a woman should be able to decide when to produce, works perfectly when forbidding children. Women can decide to forbid when they feel like it. However, there is no simple solution for women who are unable to procreate. She makes it sound so simple. Breeding thoughtlessly? A woman who has given God control of her womb should not be viewed as "breeding thoughtlessly." She is operating in faith. Well, I guess you can call that thoughtlessly, or better than that, taking no thought for tomorrow, trusting that tomorrow will take thought for the things of itself. Sufficient unto the day is the evil thereof. {Matthew 6:34}

Now, that is what I call faith! Faith <u>is</u> operating thoughtlessly. As a matter of fact, "faith is the <u>substance</u> of things <u>hoped</u> <u>for</u> and the evidence of things <u>not seen</u>."

I was thinking about First Corinthians, chapter seven. It speaks of two types of women, a married woman whose affections should be toward her husband, and a single woman, whose affections should be on the Lord to serve Him without distractions. However, Margaret views that topic like this, "Our present laws force women into one of two ways: Celibacy, with its nervous results, or abortion.

All modern physicians testify that both these conditions are harmful; that celibacy is the cause of many nervous complaints, while abortion is a disgrace to a civilized community. Physicians claim that early marriage with knowledge to control birth would do away with both."

Unfortunately, Sanger's teachings are the direct opposite of Paul's teachings, that taught young women to marry, bare children, and guide the house, according to *1Timothy 5:14*.

She also said, "Women must be protected from incessant (continuing without interruption; ceaseless; unending) childbearing before she can actively participate in the social life."

Saints, are we supposed to actively participate in the social life, or be keepers at home?

It is clear to me that Margaret Sanger's teaching reproachfully scoffed at women's true role. I cannot imagine being protected from incessant childbearing. I am thankful that I yielded my vessel and did not interrupt God's plans for my heritage. Protected is defined as, to defend or guard from attack, invasion, loss, annoyance, insult, etc.; cover shield from injury or danger. To protect a woman in that way will interfere with a man freely coming together with his wife. And that is directly against the scripture. Fasting and prayer is the only Biblical reason for separating intimately. However, there may be physical or medical reasons that will prevent intimacy.

I pray that my dear sisters are not viewing their children as an attack, invasion, loss, annoyance, insult or any such thing. As a matter of fact, we should view them as a blessing. Can I get an Amen?

{1 Corinthians 7:3-5}

3 Let the husband render unto the wife due benevolence: and likewise, also the wife unto the husband.

4 The wife hath not power of her own body, but the husband: and likewise, also the husband hath not power of his own body, but the wife.

5 Defraud ye not one the other, except it be with consent for a time, that ye may give yourselves to fasting and prayer; and come together again, that Satan tempt you not for your incontinency.

Anne Higgins, mother to Margaret Sanger, went through 18 pregnancies (with 11 live births) in 22 years before dying at age 50. Over the course of her career, Sanger was arrested, at least eight times, for expressing her views <u>during an era in which speaking publicly about contraception was illegal</u>. Wow, so it looks like even speaking openly about contraceptives was illegal. The sad thing is, the church has jumped on board and has accepted this as well. Oh my, how far have we fallen, to go from speaking about controlled birth being illegal to it being the norm, even in the Body of Christ? How did we become so free to the point of supporting birth control in the house of the Lord? Have you ever heard what one generation does in moderation the next generation does it in excess? The concept of forbidding children in the U.S began with Margaret Sanger, who is now deceased. However, Satan still has agents sowing her doctrines unawares. Unfortunately, some of these agents are members of the Body of Christ.

The following is a Testimony that it Does Still Exist.

*My name is Jacqueline Williams. I am a saved, sanctified, Holy Ghost filled woman of God. I have been married for nine years; and I am believing God to open my womb. I have not used contraceptives in almost 10 years. I have given God full control over my life and my womb. As time has progressed I have become more and more convinced that God should be in control of every aspect of my life, **INCLUDING MY WOMB**. My husband and I yearn for children. However, we both accept that God has our seed numbered. I have seen the outcomes of preventing God from having free course in our wombs. I watched my mother struggle with the effects of a tubal ligation for almost 20 years, including several blood transfusions, doctor visits, anemia and tumors that developed after her procedure. This year, after several attempts to resolve her issue, my mother had to undergo a complete hysterectomy. From this day forward, she will have to take medication to get her body to perform as it would if those organs were still intact. The doctors inform you that the tubal ligation will prevent pregnancy, however, they do not tell you of true risk and complications that I have seen unfold in my mother's life. After being with the man I love since I was nineteen, I am yearning and longing to connect on another level by bearing his child. The desire to raise a child in holiness is overwhelming at times. The church has fallen asleep in child bearing. To complain and murmur about bearing children when there is someone in your presence that would gladly take your place is insensitive at the least. I was created to bear children and to raise them in a loving and pure environment.*

Minister Jacqueline Williams

Testimonials

*I was pregnant with my last child DJ. My husband and I had decided that he would have a vasectomy. During one of my last visits my doctor and husband began to talk me into having my tubes tied. The rationale was I would already be under anesthesia and it would therefore be much easier since I would be recovering from childbirth anyway. So, I fed into it and had the procedure done. I really didn't even put much thought to it. Besides, this was something that many of my family members had done. I mean the whole reason that my husband and I even decided to do any type of birth control, was because of advice given by people we looked up to. I can remember one of the female family patriarchs telling us, "**Every time you have a baby it's a setback.**" Well I remember my son being about a month old; it really sank in what I had done. I felt an overwhelming sadness and began to cry almost inconsolably. Over the next few years it would cross my mind, and I would feel the regret of that decision. I also noticed that my cycles became more painful, and the length grew longer. I used to experience a 3 to 4-day cycle, now I noticed it was lasting 6 to 7 days. I took my concerns to my doctor, who told me that I had small uterine fibroid tumors. He suggested that I have a hysterectomy. I immediately knew within myself that this was because I had the tubal ligation. I was able to put the physician off, asking him to give me time to think about it. I ended up scheduling the hysterectomy but did not follow through. When I saw my doctor the following year for my annual female visit, he told me that I was now anemic due to my fibroids. He said the fibroids were twice as big, and that I needed to have my uterus removed as soon as possible. I decided that I would not go back to him and didn't see a doctor for the next two years. I noticed my belly began to protrude. When I went to give blood, which I did at least twice a year, I was told that I was too anemic to give blood. It was at this point I knew I needed to find a doctor that was going fix my issue without having a hysterectomy. I visited my new doctor and told her my history and explained that since I had my tubal ligation I have had problems with my cycle and now I was anemic. When they did my blood work my Iron was so low that the nurse told me she didn't know how I was walking around. After going back and forth with my doctor trying everything she could to prevent me from having the hysterectomy, it finally became apparent that I would have to have the surgery. When I went in for the surgery, before they could begin, I had to receive 2 units of blood. I came through the surgery; however, my blood was still so low that I had to receive 2 more units. I began to recover and upon discharge I noticed that I was still bleeding, deep red blood. Upon examination it was revealed that there was a tear that was causing blood loss and I was rushed back into surgery to have it repaired which resulted in two additional units of blood. I made it through by the grace and mercy of God. I believe with all that is within me, my undergoing that hysterectomy, and nearly losing my life was a result of having my tubes tied.*

Minister Shalanda T Glover

I remember when I learned that Minister G had to undergo surgery; I experienced that same inconsolable cry. I cried so hard because I knew her true heart's desire. I knew she was seeking God for a miracle. Her doctor was so sweet; she kept us posted the entire time. The doctor even took pictures of her uterus with her cell phone for us. She knew how we felt about surgery being a last result. Minister G's uterus was the size of a small soccer ball. It was covered with fibroids and had started its own blood supply. It was one of the most horrible sights you could see. Medical intervention was a miracle for her However, clipping tying and burning what freely came from God is what started her medical problems.

SEEK THE OLD PATH

"Thus saith the Lord, stand ye in the ways, and see, and ask for the old paths, where is the good way, and walk therein, and ye shall find rest for your souls. But they said; we will not walk therein."

Jeremiah 6:16

King James Bible

Seek the Old Path

"Thus saith the LORD, Stand ye in the ways, and see, and ask for the old paths, where is the good way, and walk therein, and ye shall find rest for your souls. But they said, we will not walk therein."

{*Jeremiah 6:16*}

The Lord said, *"Stand ye in the ways and ask for the old paths,"* I am doing just that. I am asking God for the old paths. I am asking for the church to understand that controlled birth was then, and still is, illegal by God's standards. I am asking for the selfishness of usurping authority over the womb to cease. I am praying for a confidence to come forth in my sisters, causing them to receive with gladness, the gift of conception.

"But they said," Jeremiah proclaimed, *"we will not walk therein. Also I set watchmen over you, saying, Hearken to the sound of the trumpet but they said, we will not hearken."* {*Jeremiah 6:16-17*}

Therefore, just as in Jeremiah's day, I know all will not hearken to this truth. However, I praise God in advance, for those who will be enlightened as I was.

18 Therefore hear, ye nations, and know, O congregation, what is among them.

19 Hear, O earth: behold, I will bring evil upon this people, even the fruit of their thoughts, because they have not hearkened unto my words, nor to my law, but rejected it.

20 To what purpose cometh there to me incense from Sheba, and the sweet cane from a far country? Your burnt offerings are not acceptable, nor your sacrifices sweet unto me."

{*Jeremiah 6:18-20*}

God is not interested in our offerings when we are not willing to obey Him in the smallest things. *"Take us the foxes, the little foxes that spoil the vines: for our vines have tender grapes."* {*Songs of Solomon 2:15*}

Please do not forbid your fruit **Women** of **God**. They are so precious and tender. Many use Planned Parenthood as an excuse to fulfill their ministry obligations. Being fruitful in marriage is a woman's first obligation.

6 Are not five sparrows sold for two farthings, and not one of them is forgotten before God?

7 But even the very hairs of your head are all numbered. Fear not therefore: ye are of more value than many sparrows."

{Luke 12:6-7}

Human value is more than many sparrows. The very hairs of our head are numbered. Does that include the heads that never part the matrix (womb) due to contraceptives? I beseech thee **Women** of **God**; let your wombs go free. Deuteronomy 32:39 says, "**See** now that I, even I, am he, and there is no god with me: I kill, and I make alive; I wound, and I heal: neither is there any that can deliver out of my hand."

Solomon's Birth {Judges 13:3-5}

3 And the angel of the LORD appeared unto the woman, and said unto her, behold now, **thou art barren**, and bearest not: but thou shalt **conceive**, and bear a son.

4 Now therefore beware, I pray thee, and drink not wine nor strong drink, and eat not any unclean thing:

5 For, lo, **thou shalt conceive**, and bear a son; and no razor shall come on his head: for the child **shall be a Nazarite unto God from the womb**: and **he shall begin to deliver Israel out of the hand of the Philistines**.

Solomon's Birth was prophesied. Just like Solomon, it is established what we will be, and what we will do before we are conceived in the womb.

DESIRE TRUTH IN
THE IN-WARD PART

Behold, Thou desirest truth in the inward parts: and in the hidden part thou shalt make me to know wisdom.... Should the truth be in that part of our body as well; the womb? Should we have truth in the pubic area?

Lady J

Desire Truth in The In-ward Part

"Shouldn't your loins be girded about with truth," asked my dear friend, Michelle. "Stand therefore, having your loins girt about with truth, and having on the breastplate of righteousness."

{Ephesians 6:14}

Loins can be identified as the area below the waist: the hips and the front of the body, considered as the part of the body that should be covered and as the site of the sexual organs. It is also considered the genital and pubic area; genitalia. Think about it ladies, "gird about." You know girdles, right? Come on now, women use girdles to hold things together. Wink! Wink! I know this is going to sound kind of weird, but should not the truth be in that part of our body as well? The womb! Should we have truth in the Pubic area? Well, you will certainly need the breast plate of righteousness to receive the truth in that part of the body. *Behold, thou desirest truth in the inward parts: and in the hidden part thou shalt make me to know wisdom. Purge me with hyssop, and I shall be clean: wash me, and I shall be whiter than snow."*

{Psalms 51:6-7}

James 1:5 reads, *"if any of you lack wisdom, let him ask of God, that giveth to all men liberally, and upbraideth not; and it shall be given him."* We need truth in our most private and secret parts. We need wisdom in our hidden parts. I encourage you to ask God for wisdom concerning conception and childbirth His way. Verse six reads, *"When you ask, ask in faith, nothing wavering. For he that wavereth is like a wave of the sea driven with the wind and tossed."*

When we waiver between what is right and what is wrong we cannot expect to receive anything from the Lord. We cannot afford to be doubled minded on this matter. James also stated, *"A double minded man is unstable in all his ways."* We just read in Jeremiah that evil would be upon the fruit of the thoughts. Do you agree that it is time to purge our thoughts? Thus, considering that His thoughts are higher than ours?

"Commit thy works unto the LORD, and thy thoughts shall be established."
{Proverbs 16:3}

If we can learn to commit our works to God in faith, our thoughts will be established, or brought into being on a firm foundation. Let us get dressed and gird up the loins of our mind, as recorded in the book of First Peter. I committed my works (having children) to God and he established my thoughts. My thoughts started to line up with the Word of God. I considered each subsequent pregnancy a blessing, it was higher than my husband and I. We could not produce offspring without God.

{1 Peter 1:13-16}

Wherefore gird up the loins of your mind, be sober, and hope to the end for the grace that is to be brought unto you at the revelation of Jesus Christ.
As obedient children, not fashioning yourselves according to the former lusts in your ignorance.
But as He which hath called you is holy, so be ye holy in all manner of conversation;
Because it is written, be ye holy; for I am holy.

WHO CHANGED
GOD OR MAN?

One big problem is too often we are being foolish and multiplying, versus being fruitful and multiplying. In other words, children are being conceived the wrong way more often than the right way. There are elder women who have two grandbabies born the wrong way and have the audacity to look down on women who have three or more for their husbands. Is that hypocrisy, or is that hypocrisy?

Lady Jay

Who Changed God or Man?

Every good and perfect gift comes from above, so who changed, God or man? Children are a gift from above and that is for sure. As a matter of fact, we can do things to stop them from coming forth, but only God can bring them forth. Controlled birth does not seem to be heard of in the Bible days. There was the one case when a man by the name of Onan spilled his seed.

7 And Er, Judah's firstborn, was wicked in the sight of the LORD; and the LORD slew him.

8 And Judah said unto Onan, go in unto thy brother's wife, and marry her, and raise up seed to thy brother.

9 And Onan knew that the seed should not be his; and it came to pass, when he went in unto his brother's wife, that he spilled it on the ground, lest that he should give seed to his brother.

10. And the thing which he did displeased the LORD: wherefore he slew him also. {Genesis 38:7-10}

Why did the Lord slay him? Some say that he died because he did not want to bring up his brother's seed. I try to take the word at face value. I cannot overlook the fact that the Bible says **"and the thing <u>which he did displeased The Lord."</u>** I had to read it slow!

What did he do? Recorded plainly in verse nine it states, when he went in unto his brother's wife, he spilled it (seed) on the ground. The why is not important. It was what he did that displeased The Lord. His actions were a result of his desire to control birth, right? Along with seed spilling, even more evil devices have been created to control birth. We must ask ourselves, "Does it displease the Lord?"

We are the temple of God. The Bible warns that whosoever defiles God's temple, God will destroy him. For the temple of God is Holy, which are ye? Birth control without a doubt defiles our temple.

{I Corinthians 3:17}

Types of birth control

The barrier method is designed to prevent sperm from entering the uterus. Examples include male and female condoms, diaphragms, cervical caps, contraceptive sponges and spermicidal. The hormonal method uses hormones to regulate or stop ovulation and prevent pregnancy. Some examples are the pill, the patch, injectable birth control; vaginal rings, implantable rods and lastly, emergency contraceptive pills. These pills can delay or inhibit ovulation for at least five days to allow sperm to be inactive.

Does that make you think of the seed Onan spilled on the ground? He seemed to know a little about what makes sperm inactive. Wink! Wink! The Intrauterine Method (The IUD) is a T shaped device that is inserted into the uterus; to prevent pregnancy. Sterilization it is a permanent form of birth control that either prevents a woman from getting pregnant; or prevents a man from releasing sperm.

The tubal ligation is a more permanent method of birth control; the fallopian tubes are closed off preventing the eggs from reaching the ovaries. {WebMD} All of the above devices were created and designed to prohibit or stop life." There are many **devices** in a <u>man's heart</u>; nevertheless, the counsel of the **LORD, THAT** shall **stand**."

{Proverbs 19:21}

Genesis 1:26-28 King James Version (KJV)

[26] And God said, let us make man in our image, after our likeness: and let them have dominion over the fish of the sea, and over the fowl of the air, and over the cattle, and over all the earth, and over every creeping thing that creepeth upon the earth.

[27] So God created man in his own image, in the image of God created he him; male and female created he them.

[28] And God blessed them, and God said unto them, Be fruitful, and multiply, and replenish the earth, and subdue it: and have dominion over the fish of the sea, and over the fowl of the air, and over every living thing that moveth upon the earth.

So God created man in his own image, in the image of God created he him; male and female created he them. And God blessed them, and God said unto them, be fruitful, and multiply, and replenish the earth, and subdue it: and have dominion over the fish of the sea, and over the fowl of the air, and over every living thing that moveth upon the earth. The counsel that God gave the first man in the beginning will stand forever. He said, "Be fruitful and multiply and replenish the earth. "I think it is embarrassing that women today stick their chest out saying, **"I ain't having all those children."**

God saw it was not good for man to be alone; so He made a help meet for him. He blessed **them,** not just him. Next, He said to **them,** not just him, "Be fruitful and multiply." "Replenish the earth, and subdue it, said the Lord. *Look at it this way; we* are called to be in submission. So, get on board married women of God, let us "**sub**" his **mission**.

Think about a certified teacher, when she has to be out, she will get a substitute right? The substitute will come in, and guide the class according to the lesson plans. Furthermore, the substitute has no business coming in changing things around; and trying to run the show. She must understand her place is, to guide things until the teacher returns.

Likewise, the head of every man is Christ, the head of woman is the man, and the head of Christ is God. "In that order." Moreover, the "**Sub**" should not usurp authority over the teacher in her absence. Neither should a woman usurp authority over man or her womb. If you only conceived one child, you have been fruitful and have multiplied.

Every woman's seed is numbered to God's pleasing and according to the number He sees fit. One big problem is too often we are being **foolish** and **multiplying**, versus being **fruitful** and **multiplying**. In other words, children are being conceived the wrong way more often than the right way. There are elder women who have two grand babies born the wrong way, and have the audacity to look down on women who have three or more for their husbands. Is that hypocrisy, or is that hypocrisy?" The Bible says, my people are destroyed for lack of knowledge: because thou hast rejected knowledge, I will also reject thee, that thou shalt be no priest to me: seeing thou hast forgotten the law of thy God, I will also forget thy children. {Hosea 4:6}

BEFORE I FORMED THEE, I KNEW THEE

Look at your favorite selfie (picture you took of yourself).
Don't be selfish; acknowledge that as sure as you are here;
every child intended for you by God should be here too.
The unborn members of birth control victims are written in
God's book as well. "Roll call", says God, is everybody here?
Unfortunately, there are quite a few members that are absent.

Lord Have Mercy!

Lady J

Before I Formed Thee, I Knew Thee

Many would agree that murder is wrong, and it stops life. Murder is defined as the unlawful premeditated killing of one human being by another, or to end life. Capital murder is the lawful infliction of death as a punishment; the death penalty stops life. Look at the horrific process of capital punishment/lethal injection.

When this method is used, the condemned person is usually bound to a gurney and a member of the execution team positions several heart monitors on the skin. Two needles (one is a back-up) are then inserted into usable veins, usually in the inmate's arms. Long tubes connect the needle through a hole in a cement block wall to several intravenous drips. The first is a harmless saline solution that is started immediately. Then, at the warden's signal, a curtain is raised exposing the inmate to the witnesses in an adjoining room. Next, the inmate is injected with sodium thiopental an anesthetic, which puts the inmate to sleep.

Next flows pavilion or pancuronium bromide, which paralyzes the entire muscle system and <u>stops the inmate's breathing</u>. Finally, the flow of potassium chloride **stops** the heart. **Death** results from anesthetic overdose and respiratory and cardiac arrest. The condemned person at that time is unconscious. {**Death Penalty Focus**}

The thought of that is horrible, isn't it? Birth control also known as contraception was designed to prevent pregnancy. What is pregnancy? Pregnancy is the fertilization and development of one or more offspring, known as an embryo or fetus, in a woman's uterus. It is the common name for gestation in humans. What is gestation? Gestation is the process of carrying or being carried in the womb between conception and birth. Now if you look at the purpose of capital punishment, **which is to stop life** by way of injection, and the purpose of birth control, **which is to prevent life** by way of injection or orally etc., what is the difference? You may say there is a big difference. Well, after reading the book of Jeremiah, I beg to differ. Let us take a closer look at what God said concerning Jeremiah. Then view it in light of the definition of murder, capital punishment/lethal injection, and the purpose of birth control.

{Jeremiah 1:4-5}

Then the word of the LORD came unto me, saying, before I formed thee in the belly I knew thee; and before thou camest forth out of the womb I sanctified thee, and I ordained thee a prophet unto the nations.

God knew Jeremiah before he was formed in the belly. He sanctified him before he came forth out of the womb. I believe this is also true concerning you and me. This is also true concerning the millions and millions of children that are blocked or murdered by contraceptives before having a chance at life. Millions of God's children are receiving "capital punishment."

They receive the death Penalty by way of contraceptives. What crime have these innocent babies committed? What wrong have they done? The fact that one can be sanctified before coming out of the womb is amazing to me. Jeremiah's purpose in life was in the heart and mind of God <u>before</u> he was even formed. That sends a chilling fear to my soul, simply because people use contraceptives so not to hinder their own personal goals or purpose in life. They are void of understanding; they cannot see that any child, intended by God, for a married man and woman is divinely predestined. Maybe you cannot receive my take on our purpose, that it was predestined before we were formed. Here is another example in the Scripture.

But he said unto them, all men cannot receive this saying, save they to whom it is given. For there are some eunuchs, which were so born from their mother's womb: and there are some eunuchs, which were made eunuchs of men: and there be eunuchs, which have made themselves eunuchs for the kingdom of heaven's sake. He that is able to receive it let him receive it.

{Matthew 19:11-12}

Verse twelve states that some eunuchs were "so born from their mother's womb." A eunuch is a man who may have been castrated; a man who is impotent, celibate or otherwise not inclined to marry or procreate. Look at castrated. Any action, surgical, chemical or otherwise a male loses use of the testes which prevents them from producing.

Consider the definition of eunuch. Is it safe to say the other percentages of men are willingly celibate or ordained to marry and multiply? I think one should make them self a eunuch. In other words, a eunuch made of men, as oppose to getting married and place stipulations on the womb.

The Processes of Life

With great wisdom, God created the cell in our body to carry on the processes of life. The cell is the smallest part of the body that is said to be alive. Because of the many tasks the cells have to carry out, they come in different sizes and shapes. The type of cell I am referring to is the sperm cell.

At birth, you contained approximately two trillion cells. However, when you began your life inside your mother's womb, you were made of only one cell. How amazing is that? God took one cell and amazingly formed you and me. It is no wonder God told Jeremiah, "Before I formed thee in the belly I knew thee." To begin as one cell and end as two trillion is baffling! Inside our mother's body, a tiny egg cell about the size of the period at the end of this sentence developed. A sperm cell, from our father's body, connected with the egg. That uniting of the egg and the sperm is called conception or beginning. In that egg God had a well packaged plan for our life.

He even established if we would be male or female. Our Heavenly Father would not ask us to do something that He is not willing or able to do Himself. He asked mankind, "to be fruitful and multiply." Likewise, that new cell from conception began to divide. Yes, it divided into two cells, then four and so forth.

The Lord is very much in to Math. After about three days, you and I looked like a ball of cells. Those cells obeyed God's commands and began to develop characteristics in structure and function. Look at your favorite selfie (Picture you took of yourself). Don't be selfish. Acknowledge that as sure as you are here, every child intended for you by God should be here, too.

Psalms 139:13-18

13. For thou hast possessed my reins: thou hast covered me in my mother's womb. 14. I will praise thee; for I am fearfully and wonderfully made: marvellous are thy works; and that my soul knoweth right well. 15. My substance was not hid from thee, when I was made in secret, and curiously wrought in the lowest parts of the earth. 16. Thine eyes did see my substance yet being unperfect; and in thy book all my members were written, which in continuance were fashioned, when yet there was none of them.

17. How precious also are thy thoughts unto me, O God! How great is the sum of them! 18. if I should count them, they are more in number than the sand: when I awake, I am still with thee.

"Hold up! Praise break!" Those verses of scriptures make me say, "Hallelujah!" My Substance was not hid from God when I was made in secret; the same applies to our children. All our members were written in his book before we were even fashioned. Likewise, the birth control victim's, though forbidden to come forth, their members are written in God's book as well. "Roll call" say's God, "Is everybody here?"

Unfortunately, there are quite a few members that are absent. Lord Have mercy! Please walk in accountability when it comes to your seed. We should not shoot hooky from our responsibilities? Pray this prayer with me: Here I am, here I stand, Lord my life is in your hand. Lord I am longing to see your desires revealed in me. I give myself away. Take my heart. Take my life, as a living sacrifice. All my dreams, all my plans, Lord I place them in your hands. My life is not my own, to you I belong. I give myself to you. I give myself away. Beautiful, simply beautiful! Those words are lyrics to the song, I give myself away. Lord knows we need to place our plans in God's hands.

It is the desire for uninterrupted plans that cause women to take birth control. My life is not my own; therefore, I surrender every part of my body to the owner himself Jesus Christ the Righteous. Naturally if your child was locked outside you would let them in, right? Well, if we are enjoying intimacy while avoiding children by way of birth control, it is no different than keeping your child locked out of the house. **Lord Help Us to take the lock off of our wombs.**

FORBID THEM NOT

Does forbid mean forbid? If Jesus said "Suffer little children to come unto Him and forbid them not," then forbidding children by way of contraceptives is just as wrong. Amen! Jesus said, "Suffer children to come" but many feel they are suffering because of them coming. Did the Church buy a lie? My Bible says buy the truth and sell it not.

Lady J

Forbid Them Not

Look at another interesting point in Matthew 19:13-14.

13 Then were there brought unto him little children that he should put his hands on them, and pray: and the disciples rebuked them.

14 But Jesus said, suffer little children, and forbid them not, to come unto me: for of such is the kingdom of heaven.

I strive to build my points on a sure foundation, The Word of God. Our Lord, is known for taking something natural, to convey a spiritual point. In the above verses, we find Jesus' disciples (his inner circle) rebuked children that were brought to the Lord. Jesus replied, "Suffer little children, and forbid them not to come unto me: He said, "Of such is the kingdom of heaven." In like manner, we discovered through Jeremiah; that God had plans for him before conception.

It seems that forbidding our children by way of contraceptives is man's way of preventing God's will "on earth as it is in Heaven." Forbid is defined as" to command (a person) not to do something, have something, etc., or not to enter some place: to prohibit something."

Does not forbid mean forbid? If He said, "suffer little children to come unto Him and forbid them not," then forbidding children by way of contraceptives is just as wrong. Amen! Jesus said, "**Suffer** **children** **to** **come**" but many feel they are **suffering as a** **result of them coming**. Did the church buy a lie? My Bible says, "Buy the truth and sell it not." {Proverbs 23:23}

No kidding, I just received a text while editing this. This is what it reads, "Talk about Conception God's Way: I met a lady today who is 54 years old and pregnant with her first child. Yes, I said age 54." My Lord! Thanks Sister Foxx your timing was impeccable, and I know you are super encouraged by that!

Testimonial

My name is Sister Seretha Bass. By the time I was twenty-one years old, I was married with three children. I was told three children were enough and that I needed to have my tubes tied. After I had my youngest daughter I started getting the Depo shot for birth control until time for my procedure. That was in 1994, when I lived in Lucedale Mississippi. I did not have a relationship with the Lord at the time. In 2003 I got married again, and three months later I received the gift of the Holy Ghost. The church that I was attending at the time started to turn away from the standards of holiness and began to compromise. Therefore, I was not being taught to be fruitful and multiply. I was led by the Spirit to leave that church, because I was not growing spiritually. I had really become stagnated. I joined Manna Ministries Inc. in the year of 2009. My pastor, Barry Jones, Sr. and his wife taught us that children should be conceived through marriage, and that women should not take birth control. I also noticed in this church the women were being fruitful in childbirth. I thought it was beautiful. I began to feel convicted now that I was a part of a ministry who taught that being fruitful was the right thing to do. I began making phone calls to Lucedale, MS. I had to find the doctor who performed my surgery. I was successful and also obtained a copy of my medical records. In 2010 I found a doctor here in Mobile who performed my tubal reversal. He explained that I had scarring, and one of my tubes was longer than the other. Therefore, I had a 60 to 70 percent chance of getting pregnant. I was confident and had faith that my God would open my womb. Four years later July 28, 2014 I found out that I was pregnant. Glory to God! Before I found out, He gave me dreams back to back, revealing that I would conceive a child. God did just what he said He would do. Glory hallelujah! I am so thankful for answered prayers. **Praise God with Sister Seretha, who forbad children at first, but later got a revelation of the truth as described in her testimony.**

OPENING/CLOSING
OF THE WOMB:
GOD'S TIMING

And when Rachel saw that she bare no children, Rachel envied her sister; and said unto Jacob give me children else I die. I love Rachel's passion for multiplication, but she had the same misconception that many have today. She thought man was in control of conception and childbirth.

Lady J

Opening/Closing of the Womb: God's Timing

Look at a story in the book of Genesis. Leah and Rachel seem to have been in competition for their husband's love, so they continued to multiply until their womb closed on its own.

30 And he went in also unto Rachel, and he loved also Rachel more than Leah, and served with him yet seven other years.

31 And when the LORD saw that Leah was hated, he opened her womb: but Rachel was barren.

32 And Leah conceived, and bare a son, and she called his name Reuben: for she said, Surely the LORD hath looked upon my affliction; now therefore my husband will love me.

33 And she conceived again, and bare a son; and said, Because the LORD hath heard I was hated, he hath therefore given me this son also: and she called his name Simeon.

34 And she conceived again, and bare a son; and said, Now this time will my husband be joined unto me, because I have born him three sons: therefore was his name called Levi.

35 And she conceived again, and bare a son: and she said, Now will I praise the LORD: therefore she called his name Judah; and left bearing. {Genesis 29:30-35}

Now consider this powerful revelation. Note that Jacob had begun an intimate relationship with Leah, yet she did not conceive. Only when The Lord saw that she was hated then he opened her womb. It seems to me, that the Lord has his own personal reason for opening and closing wombs. Remember how you learned about opposites early in life: up/down, high/low, in/out and open/closed. Her womb was closed until the Lord saw fit. Leah's womb was closed but Rachel's womb was barren. Barren is defined as, not fruiting: producing no fruit or seed; not producing or incapable of producing offspring; sterile: a barren woman, Unproductive; unfruitful: Unable to have children: not able to bear children. The Bible records that Leah conceived four sons and then she left bearing. It is high time for the body of Christ to trust the God of Abraham, Isaac, and Jacob. We must understand that every womb will leave bearing at His appointed time.

He also specializes in opening wombs as well. And when Rachel saw that she bare Jacob no children, Rachel envied her sister; and said unto Jacob, give me children, or else I die. And Jacob's anger was kindled against Rachel: and he said, am I in God's stead, who hath withheld from thee the fruit of the womb? {Genesis 30:1-2}

I love Rachel's passion for multiplication, but on the contrary, she seemed to have the same misconception that many have today. She thought man was in control of conception and childbirth.

Considering Jacob loved Rachel more than he loved Leah, if it were in his power he probably would have given her as many children as she wanted. Jacob was angered by the thought of this woman he loved so dearly thinking conception and childbirth was in his hands or in his power. *"Am I in God's stead, who hath withheld from thee the fruit of the womb," He asked?*

Jacob understood that it was The Lord withholding her womb. He asked, "Am I in God's stead?" I am feeling compelled to express; that too many saints have placed themselves in God's stead when it comes to their womb. Stead is defined as the place, position, or function. When it comes to the fruit of the womb this area or position is for God alone to govern. We should not stand in His stead. Rachel gave her handmaiden to Jacob out of desperation for multiplication. Likewise, when Leah saw that she had left bearing; she took Zillah her maid and gave her Jacob to wife.

Leah patterned after Rachel and gave her spouse to her maid also. She realized her womb was resting. I chose the word "**resting**" because just like when we take a natural rest or nap, by the grace of God we wake up again. Leah's womb did just that. It awakened, or should I say opened again, causing her to birth three more children. This time around it was two boys and a baby girl. So, God picks the gender also. Wow! I am reminded of when I was asked as a teenager how many children I wanted, I would say two: a boy and girl. As if it really worked like that! God's thoughts were certainly higher than mine on that one. I have eleven beautiful babies. One day I was out running errands.

I overheard a conversation that went like this, "Well, we had two girls and we said we were done." "Then my wife decided she wanted another girl, of course it was a boy." {Decided she wanted} It was Wishful thinking huh? I think we have all had those moments that we realize some things are not in our control. I am so thankful for a sweet mother in the Lord. Can we call her Mother D? She had five children, and ten years later she had her sixth child. She did not use birth control. It looks like God is certainly good at controlling birth.

Mother D left her womb for the Lord to govern. The Lord "jump started" Mother D's womb again. Her sixth child, we can call her Sister Y.F. The Lord did not stop there; Mother D had two more babies after Sister Y.F. Yes, that is a grand total of eight children, plus one in Heaven that did not make it. Oh, did I mention grown children?

Let us not forget the patriarch, Mr. D who fathered her children. They were married for over sixty years until death recently caused them to part. Now, that is the old path. She had five children, then ten years later here comes Sister Y.F. Now that my friend, is birth control! She was a woman who left her womb for the Lord to control.

Sister YF has been married eleven years. Ironically, that is a little over the time that had elapsed upon her conception and birth. She has not conceived as of yet. Like Rachel, if saying or doing something could bring a baby to her arms, trust me Sister Y.F. would have filled that desire years ago. Truthfully, if it were in my power I would give her a child myself. However, I realize like Jacob, that I am not in God's stead. Consider this, God closed Mother D's womb for ten years. A miracle in the person of Sister Y.F. arrives. My God is more than able to visit Sister Y.F. womb after more than ten years of marriage has passed. Hallelujah! On that note, anyone who has been freely given an open womb from the Lord should think twice and three times over before selling it out to birth control. Amen!

It's the truth anyhow

Ok, I surrender Sister Y.F. is Sister Foxx who sent me the text message earlier. God is good.

Fruitful & Multiply

A Man and his wife should freely receive the gift of conception and teach their children to embrace the fruit of the womb as well. Remember says God, Before I formed thee in the belly I knew thee! The pregnant belly should be embraced not looked upon as a disgrace.

Amen!

KNOWING THE
THINGS FREELY GIVEN
TO US FROM GOD

`It is of utmost importance for us to understand that being able to conceive a child is freely given to us of God! We should be aware of everything in this life that is given to us of God. We should know the things that are impossible with man, and only possible through God.

Lady J

Knowing the Things Freely Given to Us by God

Take a look at conception and childbirth through the light of I Corinthians 2:9-16.

9 But as it is written, Eye hath not seen, nor ear heard, neither have entered into the heart of man, the things which God hath prepared for them that love him.

10 But God hath revealed them unto us by his Spirit: for the Spirit searcheth all things, yea, the deep things of God.

11 For what man knoweth the things of a man save the spirit of man which is in him? Even so the things of God knoweth no man, but the Spirit of God.

12 Now we have received, not the spirit of the world, but the spirit which is of God; that we might know the things that are freely given to us of God.

13 Which things also we speak, not in the words which man's wisdom teacheth, but

14 which the Holy Ghost teacheth; comparing spiritual things with spiritual.

15 But the natural man receiveth not the things of the Spirit of God: for they are foolishness unto him: neither can he know them, because they are spiritually discerned.

16 But he that is spiritual judgeth all things, yet he himself is judged of no man. For who hath known the mind of the Lord, that he may instruct him? But we have the mind of Christ.

Be honest, does it not bring joy to your heart and to your mind, that God already prepared everything pertaining to life and Godliness for those who love Him? This brings me back to a point I made earlier. This concept would not carry weight to the world, but with the church. Considering we have not received the spirit of the world, but the Spirit which is of God, our thinking should be different. God's thoughts are higher than ours; therefore, our thoughts should certainly be higher than the world's.

Many saints will find themselves in trouble with God trying to instruct Him when it comes to family planning. Let's pray that we may know the things that are freely given to us of God." The fact that you must medically disable or prevent life, which comes freely from God, tells me all I need to know about birth control. I boldly proclaim that family planning is straight from the enemy of our soul. Mankind should never intentionally think for God. His thoughts are higher than our thoughts.

"8 For my thoughts are not your thoughts, neither are your ways my ways, saith the LORD".

9 For as the heavens are higher than the earth, so are my ways higher than your ways, and my thoughts than your thoughts." {Isaiah 55:8-9}

It is of utmost importance for us to understand that being able to conceive a child is freely given to us of God! We should be aware of everything in this life that is given to us of God. We should know the things that are impossible with man, and only possible through God. Too many Christians are evaluating their information according to fleshly reasoning, carnal desires, and man's wisdom; instead of what the Holy Ghost teaches.

The Scripture says it perfectly, "14 But the <u>natural man receiveth not the things of the Spirit of God: for they are foolishness unto him: neither can he know them, because they are spiritually discerned</u>."

{1 Corinthians 2:14}

Pray to the Almighty God and ask Him to show you how He really feels about this topic." It is clear to me that the subject of family planning is spiritually discerned. Let us remember he that is spiritual judgeth all things. Remember to judge righteous judgment. It behooves us to be very sure in judging controlled birth righteously. I dread becoming the type of saint that rejects subjects that does not begin with, "Thou shalt not" in the Bible.

The best example I can give is Balaam's story found in Numbers 22:18-23. I believe God expects us to know his mind-set when it comes to certain things. As saints, we should know how to possess our members with sanctification and honor.

We must take a stand on what is right in the face of wrong and worldly influences. We cannot bow down to an era where the majority rules and anything goes. Balak wanted Balaam to come and curse the people of God. He promised him great honor. Balaam was very direct with his response; he said, "If Balak gives me his house full of silver and gold, I cannot go beyond the word of the Lord my God, to do less or more." How many of us sing I'd rather have Jesus than silver and gold?

Can we still sing that song when the test of time comes? When truth knocks on the door, will we open it or close it fast? God came unto Balaam and said, "If the servants come to call you, rise up and go with them." God said, "The word that I shall say unto you that shalt thou do."

Sadly, Balaam got up the next morning and went to the princess of Moab. He should have let them come to him as God instructed. Likewise, the church is going to the world for counsel instead of letting them come to us for Biblical truth. The Bible says, God was angry because Balaam went. On top of that, the angel of the Lord stood in the way for an adversary against him. He was perfect in his ways to seek God about the matter. After everything the Lord said, Balaam's own will only allowed him to hear "go." Beloved, many of us, like Balaam, have determined not to go beyond the Word of the Lord. Unfortunately, we have done just that with the subject of birth control.

The donkey was trying to help Balaam see that he was in error. I can imagine Balaam was thinking, this old donkey is distracting me. He hit the donkey three times, trying to press his way in the wrong direction. I know many may feel I am a donkey for what I am implying. I do not mind because I have had many prenatal beatings. I know without a shadow of doubt that being fruitful is the will of God.

{*Isaiah 5:20-23*}

20 Woe unto them that call evil good, and good evil; that put darkness for light, and light for darkness; that put bitter for sweet, and sweet for bitter!

21 Woe unto them that are wise in their own eyes, and prudent in their own sight!

22 Woe unto them that are mighty to drink wine, and men of strength to mingle strong drink: Which justify the wicked for reward and take away the righteousness of the righteous from him!

It is high time for the church to look at this topic of conception and childbirth His (Christ) way. There is no chapter, book or verse to support the idea of controlled birth. However, it is my goal to build a foundation on the topic of being fruitful and multiplying. I pray that you will draw an informed conclusion. Hopefully, by His spirit we will know if numbering our seed is optional or to be left for the God's discretion. Isaiah said, "Woe unto them that call evil good and good evil; that put darkness for light and light for darkness."

There should be a clear distinction between clean and unclean and between holy and unholy. We must seriously guard against putting darkness for light and light for darkness. As thou knowest not what is the way of the Spirit, nor how the bones do grow in the womb of her that is with child: even so thou knowest not the works of God who maketh all. {Ecclesiastes 11:5} What a beautiful concept. Too often in the body of Christ, we act as if we have a diploma when it comes to the **Spirit** of God.

The above verse declares "as thou knowest not the way of the spirit, nor how the bones do grow in the womb of her that is with child." Consider this thought: you and I, along with the rest of the world can trace our beginning to a liquid secretion. A seed is found in whom we know as our natural father. From that seed through God we live, move and have our being as recorded in Acts 17:28. That alone should cause us to take conception and childbirth a little more seriously. Look at the liquid in a glass you are drinking from. How do you go from something equivalent to that: to walking, talking, living and breathing?

Since we marvel, and are unsure of how bones grow, or the growth process of an unborn child in the womb, it seems unwise to number our seed or forbid conception of the womb in any way.

22 For as I passed by, and beheld your devotions, I found an altar with this inscription, TO THE UNKNOWN GOD. Whom therefore ye ignorantly worship, him declare I unto you.

*23 **God that made the world and all things therein**, seeing that he is Lord of heaven and earth, dwelleth not in temples made with hands;*

*24 Neither is worshipped with men's hands, as though he needed anything, seeing **he giveth to all life**, and breath, and all things;*

*25 And hath made of one blood all nations of men for to dwell on all the face of the earth, and **hath determined the times before appointed**, and the bounds of their habitation;*

26 That they should seek the Lord, if haply they might feel after him, and find him, though he be not far from every one of us:

*27 **For in him we live, and move, and have our being**; as certain also of your own poets have said, For **we are also his offspring**.*

*28 Forasmuch then as we are the offspring of God, **we ought not to think that the Godhead is like unto gold, or silver, or stone, graven by art and man's device**.*

*29 And the times of this ignorance God **winked** at; but now **commandeth all men everywhere to repent**:*

*30 Because he hath appointed a day, in the which **he will judge the world in righteousness** by that man whom he hath ordained; whereof he hath given assurance unto all men, in that he hath raised him from the dead.*

Look at verse 24 again, "And hath made of one blood all nations of men for to dwell on all the face of earth, and hath determined the times before appointed, and the bounds of their habitation." This reminds me of the creation of the first man Adam; God had **all** of us in mind. One blood line is responsible for my very being. **All** generations of mankind are God's handy work and appointed before our time. Believe it or not, even the children blocked by contraception.

Our existence was appointed before the foundation of the world. We must seek Him if haply we might feel after Him and find Him. Beloved, be encouraged and understand He is not far from every one of us. The Bible says, "Draw nigh unto God, and He will draw nigh unto you. Ecclesiastes 12:13 says, "The whole duty of man is to fear God and keep his commandments." For in Him we live move and have our being." If it is okay for me to be here, who am I to determine how many children I will <u>tolerate</u>? Can you hear what the Spirit is saying to the church? Can you hear the Spirit saying, "Make a change?"

GRACIOUSLY
GIVEN BY GOD

I cannot count how many times my husband and I was asked, "Are you all done?" "How many are y'all going to have?" "When are you going to stop?" My husband's reply is, "I was number ten.' "Had my mom stopped from one through nine, I would not be here."

Lady J

Graciously Given by God

It's appears, from the beginning, it was the perfect will of God for us to be under His complete leadership in every area of our life, even in the bedroom. It is of most importance that we realize He gives life. We are His offspring. Would it not be awesome if the church would learn from our forefathers? The Bible says, in <u>Proverbs</u> <u>22:28,</u> "Remove not the ancient landmark, which thy fathers have set." Would it not be wonderful if we viewed conception and childbirth as a **reward**? Look at Jacobs's mindset towards his children.

Genesis 33:4-7

And Esau ran to meet him, and embraced him, and fell on his neck, and kissed him: and they wept. And he lifted up his eyes, and saw the women and the children; and said who are those with thee? And he said, the children which God hath graciously given thy servant. Then the handmaidens came near, they and their children, and they bowed themselves. And Leah also with her children came near and bowed themselves: and after came Joseph near and Rachel, and they bowed themselves.

{Genesis 48 8-16}

Esau saw the women and children, but for some reason Jacob only acknowledged the children who he felt were given to him graciously from God. I was truly amazed when I found that many years had passed, Jacob had gotten old and his eyes were dim. His son Joseph felt the same way about his children. *And Israel beheld Joseph's sons, and said,* <u>Who are these?</u> *And Joseph said unto his father,* **<u>They are my sons, whom God hath given</u>** **<u>me in this place</u>**. *And he said, bring them, I pray thee, unto me, and* **<u>I will bless them</u>**. *Now the eyes of Israel were dim for age, so that he could not see. And he brought them near unto him; and* **<u>he kissed them</u>**, *and embraced them. And Israel said unto Joseph,* **<u>I had not thought to see thy</u>** **<u>face: and, lo, God hath shewed me also thy seed.</u>** *And Joseph brought them out from between his knees, and he bowed himself with his face to the earth.*

And Joseph took them both, Ephraim in his right hand toward Israel's left hand, and Manasseh in his left hand toward Israel's right hand and brought them near unto him. And Israel stretched out his right hand, and laid it upon Ephraim's head, who was the younger, and his left hand upon Manasseh's head, guiding his hands wittingly; for Manasseh was the firstborn. And he blessed Joseph, and said, God, before whom my father's Abraham and Isaac did walk, **<u>the God which fed me all my life long unto this day.</u>**

*The Angel which redeemed me from all evil, **bless the lads**; and let my name be named on them, and the name of my father's Abraham and Isaac; and **let them grow into a multitude in the midst of the earth**. {Genesis 48 8-16}*

Wow, like father like son! Years down the line, the son felt the same way. He felt the children were given to him by God. What is truly astonishing, Joseph only had two children compared to his Father who had twelve sons and one daughter. I think the Bible is right and somebody is wrong! Pastor Barry Jones Sr says it like this, "any revelation we get, or level of assurance should be measured next to the Word of God. If anything gets dropped, please let it not be the Word of God". Israel was honored to not only see Jacob but his seed as well. He told Joseph to let his seed grow into a multitude. Do you trust that God will feed you and yours all your life? If you believe that, let your seed grow into a multitude in the midst of the earth.

Our God pays child support on time and every time. He does not have arrears when it comes to our family. **He definitely owes no back pay**. So, what does the Lord think about conception and childbirth? We can find the answer in the Word of God.

*Lo, **children** are an **heritage** of the LORD: and the fruit of the womb is his **reward**. As arrows are in the hand of a mighty man; so are children of the youth. Happy is the man that hath his quiver full of them: **they shall not be ashamed**, but they shall speak with the enemies in the gate.*

{Psalms 127:3-5}

Let us dissect that. A reward is defined as a thing given in recognition of one's service, efforts, or achievement. Another definition is to make a gift of something to someone. If we carefully consider the term reward, we realize everyone does not necessarily receive a reward. When a reward is received, it is for a certain purpose as well a certain or appointed time. The person giving the award determines that purpose and the time. I remember when I took on the challenge of taking college classes. On top of being married to a pastor, and having seven children, I was pregnant with twins. Two of my classes were online which consumed a concentrated amount of time. I was also studying for and passed my insurance exam. I wear many hats, I was thrilled to maintain and balance that season of my life.

One of the spectacular highlights of that season was the fact that I received a reward in my English class. The reason for that reward was that I maintained an A average the entire semester. Wow! How exciting! The **rewarder** was my professor Dr. Odom. She made that determination, and it was appointed for that semester and time. Every other semester, prior or afterward, would have to speak for itself. My point is... Every child is given by our Heavenly Father. He is our **rewarder**.

Each child is for God's purpose, as it was with Jeremiah. God even determines the season and the appointed time. That brings me to the comments like, "Why are you having them so close together? "That is not good for your health." Maybe it is, maybe it is not, but I do know this, a man and his wife can come together every day, several times a day, but only God can determine the time for seed. Therefore, children are a heritage of the Lord. Heritage: something that comes or belongs to one by reason of birth; an inherited lot or portion: Something reserved for one: Many people are waiting for their heritage due to them upon the death of a love one. However, The Bible says, Children are a heritage of the Lord, or from the Lord, but **people** have a problem with that. If something were to suddenly change about the amount of your natural heritage, would you search diligently to see why? So, why is it so different for your heritage from God Himself? The fruit of the womb is His reward.

Who would not accept a reward from God? Not any one in their right mind. However, if our understanding is unfruitful, we will reject His rewards unawares. I mentioned earlier that I had two online classes. On the first day of class my Psychology teacher asked all students to introduce themselves via the web. He said, tell everyone about you.

The way the class was set up, he would ask a question; and all of us had to respond to get a grade. Of course, I introduced myself as a mother of seven, pregnant with twins. That obviously cooked his goose (irritated him). Several days later, his question of the day was, "**How many children should people have; and what factors should be considered?**" Wow! Well, along with many other words, my response was, "This is a very disrespectful question."

I continued, "If anyone in this class lists any number under nine, you are boldly telling me my children have no right to be here." I exclaimed, "There are no factors to be considered; unless of course, you are conceiving children out of wedlock." Let me just say, every time I logged in, there was not one response from my classmates. My teacher never said another word either. Can you believe this guy? I dropped that class. That professor and many others try to make women feel **ashamed** for having multiple children. However, as I said, the Bible is right, and somebody is wrong.

Once again the Bible says... Lo, children are a heritage of the Lord: and the fruit of the womb is His reward. As arrows are in the hand of a mighty man; so are children of the youth. Happy is the man that hath his quiver full of them: they shall not be **ashamed**, but the shall speak with the enemies in the gate.

Psalms 127:3-5

All I am saying is, if you let your womb free and only two are freely giving to you of God, your quiver is full. Just be willing to have as many as **God allows**. The Bible says, "We will not be ashamed, but will speak to the enemy in the gate." I cannot count how many times my husband and I were asked, "Are you all done? How many are you going to have? When are you going to stop?" My husband's reply is, "I was number ten.' "Had my mom stopped from one through nine, I would not be here." **Now, that is so true?**

I must say, the worst question by far was, **"Does your husband ever let you up for air?"** Believe it or not, that question was from a <u>Pastor</u>.

<u>LORD HAVE MERCY</u>!

A VISIT FROM THE LORD

See the truth is, there is a set time for you and I to conceive and bear children. If Sarah understood that, I'm sure she would not have gotten ahead of God; but waited patiently for the Lord's timing. I submit to you, there is no need for birth control. It is for certain that God himself controls birth very well.

Lady J

A Visit from the Lord

Look at this revelation from the Bible. Although married to the same man, Pen-ni-nah had children, but Hannah had no children. The Lord had shut up Hannah's womb. Women in the Bible day appeared grieved when they were not able to conceive. El-Ka-nah did not seem to understand his wife's desperation. He assumed his love and provision would fill that void of her longing for a child. **His response to her dilemma was**, "Am I not better to thee than ten sons." His words did not relieve her of the great sadness she felt. She eventually prayed unto the Lord and wept sore.

Hannah vowed to God that if He blesses her with a son, she will give him right back for His service. You know the story. Because she spoke in her heart and only her lips moved, with no words heard, Eli thought she was drunk. Just think about that. She prayed so fervently that she appeared to be drunk. Please do not misinterpret me. By no means am I saying that all fervent prayers will end with a testimony like Hannah's. We know that is not the truth. Think about women all over the world who like Hannah, wish they had at least one child to hold and to call their own. Once Eli understood the abundance of Hannah's grief, he spoke a blessing over her life. *Then Eli answered and said, go in peace: and the God of Israel grants thee thy petition that thou hast asked of him.*

{1 Samuel 1:17}

His words restored her countenance. She was no longer sad. The next time El-ka-nah came together with Hannah, the Lord remembered her. That is so beautiful. The Lord remembered her as He did Rachel. He opened her womb. Rachel conceived and bares a son, and her response was, "**God hath taking away my reproach**.

{Genesis 30:22-23}

And God remembered Rachel, and God hearkened to her, and opened her womb. And she conceived, and bare a son; and said, God hath taken away my reproach:

Just a little after conceiving Joseph Rachel proclaimed, "The Lord shall add unto me another son." How did we get here? How did we go from women feeling reproached when they could not conceive, to women feeling reproached at the thought of conceiving? Hannah named her first son Samuel saying, "Because I have asked him of the Lord." After weaning the child, she did just as she vowed, Hannah gave him to the Lord. Upon the arrival of the child to the temple, Eli once again spoke a blessing over the couple. He told El-Ka-nah and Hannah that "the Lord was going to give them a child, for the child that was loaned to God."

{1Samuel 2:21}

21 And the LORD <u>visited</u> **Hannah**, so that she conceived, and bare three sons and two daughters. And the child Samuel grew before the LORD."

Testimonial

I thank my Lord and Savior Jesus Christ for blessing me with a best friend that love God. Elect-Lady Jones loves God, and not only ministers His Word but lives it. She believes the whole book. My testimony I must say, took place seventeen years ago. My son name is Vincent Jacori who we call Tre (my husband called him boom as a little boy). After years of trying to conceive, I made up my mind that I would adopt a child. I had testing done to find out why we had not conceived, and every test came back negative. Therefore, the thought entered my mind that it was not God's will. My husband's response to the thought of adoption was "Let's not talk about it." About a month later I was very sick not realizing why. All I know is I had never felt so bad. I stayed in bed all day with a tooth ache. The following week I took a pregnancy test and sure enough it was positive. I believe when we get out of God's way, He can move. We must learn to let go and let God. I can remember working my entire pregnancy. One Thursday night coming home I looked in the sky, there was a full moon. I started praying and said, "I give this child to you Lord not in death but to serve you." God gave me a blessing and I gave him back to the Lord. (Hannah) The next morning I went in labor and after twenty-three hours and twenty minutes I delivered naturally a nine-pound four-ounce baby boy. He was born at 4:20am September 20.

I know God is about family and natural childbirth because every time the anesthesiologist would try and give me an epidural it would not work. I felt the pain and delivered a healthy child. Sometime later, I read in the scripture how God told Israel to dedicate to him all males that open the matrix. He wanted the first fruit, the strength, and the best. Do God a favor; do it His way!

Prophetess Marion Collins

What a testimony! I think it is amazing how Prophetess Collins and her husband tried and tried. She even considered adoption. But as she revealed in her testimony, conception and childbirth is in God's time, so we might as well do it His way. If every Christian woman could hear my voice, and I ask; "By show of hands, who would like for the Lord to pay you a visit?" I am sure every single hand will go up.

It would be wonderful if women of today viewed conception and childbirth as a visit from the Lord? I know every person breathing would appreciate the Lord paying them a visit, for one reason or another. What about your womb? Will you allow the Lord to visit your womb? Has the Lord already come by to visit your womb, but the dead-bolt lock of contraceptives had it barricaded? Who would intentionally barricade the Lord in any form? A true Christian would not.

The Bible says, "My people are destroyed for lack of knowledge: because thou hast rejected knowledge, I will also reject thee, that thou shalt be no priest to me: seeing thou hast forgotten the law of thy God, I will also forget thy children." {Hosea 4:6}

God said, "Because you forgot my law, I will also forget your children. That makes me think of those who have such a hard time conceiving after faithfully taking their contraceptives. There are consequences for going against the grain. If God purposed to say, I will forget your children, I think our children should at least be in the earth realm. I think we should readily have as many children as God allows. I also feel we should raise them to fear Him so He want forget them. I believe the Lord is visiting many Christian women's wombs, but He is not welcomed. Do not enter they say. I'm in college. I'm not financially able. My nerves are too bad. I don't want all those children.

There are many excuses for not letting the Lord number our seed according to His will. Sarah received a special visit from the Lord years prior to Hannah's visit.

1And the LORD visited Sarah as he had said, and the LORD did unto Sarah as he had spoken.

2 For Sarah conceived, and bare Abraham a son in his old age, at the set time of which God had spoken to him. {Genesis 21:1-2}

This is a powerful story, as it proves that God visits the womb when He is ready.

After these things the word of the LORD came unto Abram in a vision, saying, Fear not, Abram: I am thy shield, and thy exceeding great reward.

And Abram said, LORD God, what wilt thou give me, seeing I go childless, and the steward of my house is this Eliezer of Damascus?

And Abram said, Behold, to me thou hast given no seed: and, lo, one born in my house is mine heir.

And, behold, the word of the LORD came unto him, saying, this shall not be thine heir; but he that shall come forth out of thine own bowels shall be thine heir.

And he brought him forth abroad, and said, look now toward heaven, and tell the stars, if thou be able to number them: and he said unto him, so shall thy seed be.

And he believed in the LORD; and he counted it to him for righteousness.

{Genesis 15:1-6}

Abraham was concerned because, at this point in his life, he was still childless. God plainly explained that he was going to give Abraham seed, and He said, His seed will be as the stars in the sky. Abraham believed in the Lord, but his wife Sar-ai, had a little faith issue.

Here we find another situation of desperation. However, it unfortunately did not transpire as smoothly as Hannah's testimony. Hannah went to the Lord in prayer while Sar-ai went to her handmaid for resolution.

1 Now Sarai Abram's wife bare him no children: and she had a handmaid, an Egyptian, whose name was Hagar.

2 And Sarai said unto Abram, behold now, the LORD hath restrained me from bearing: I pray thee, go in unto my maid; it may be that I may obtain children by her. And Abram hearkened to the voice of Sarai.

3 And Sarai Abram's wife took Hagar her maid the Egyptian, after Abram had dwelt ten years in the land of Canaan and gave her to her husband Abram to be his wife.

4 And he went in unto Hagar, and she conceived: and when she saw that she had conceived, her mistress was despised in her eyes. {Genesis 16:1-4}

Remember, God said, "He that is from thy own bowels shall be thine heir." Ishmael was from Abraham bowels, but he was not the heir whom God was referring to.

And God said unto Abraham, as for Sarai thy wife, thou shalt not call her name Sarai, but Sarah shall her name be.

And I will bless her and give thee a son also of her: yea, I will bless her, and she shall be a mother of nations; kings of people shall be of her.

Then Abraham fell upon his face, and laughed, and said in his heart, shall a child be born unto him that is an hundred years old? and shall Sarah, that is ninety years old, bear?

And Abraham said unto God, O that Ishmael might live before thee!

And God said, Sarah thy wife shall bear thee a son indeed; and thou shalt call his name Isaac: and I will establish my covenant with him for an everlasting covenant and with his seed after him.

And as for Ishmael, I have heard thee: Behold, I have blessed him, and will make him fruitful, and will multiply him exceedingly; twelve princes shall he beget, and I will make him a great nation.

But my covenant will I establish with Isaac, which Sarah shall bear unto thee at this set time in the next year.

And he left off talking with him, and God went up from Abraham. {Genesis 17:15-22}

Abraham seemed to have lost sight on God's promise as well. He said, "Oh that Ishmael might walk before thee." God assured Abraham that Ishmael was going to be blessed, fruitful and that he would multiply. "But my covenant," said God, "will be with Isaac, which Sar-ah shall bear unto thee at this set time the next year, is what God assured Abraham.

See the truth is there is a set time for you and me to conceive and bear children. If Sarah understood that, I am sure she would not have gotten ahead of God but would have waited patiently for the Lord's timing. I submit to you, there is no need for birth control. It is for certain that God Himself controls birth very well. Think about it, Sarah's womb is restrained and not able to conceive while her maid immediately became pregnant from the same man. Sarah felt that she had a dilemma which she was responsible for solving. The Lord restrained her from bearing, yet He promised her husband would be a father.

She, looking at her natural state, never saw herself being the person through whom this covenant child would be birthed. She was looking in the natural. Sarah was thinking carnally like the women of today. We should remember that, "to be carnally minded is death but to be spiritually minded is life and peace." To fix what appeared to be a problem, Sarah ordered her husband to go in unto her maid. Sarah's poor decision making had consequences. Hagar began to despise her. Even though it was Sarah's idea, she blamed Abraham for the sufferings she had to bare when it came to Hagar. God had a set time for her to conceive.

{Genesis 21:1-2}

Remember, Abraham believed in the Lord and it was counted as righteousness. I submit it is absolute lack of faith and unbelief that causes one to take birth control. I have a question. Will that be counted for unrighteousness? Do you remember I said earlier, we must be aware of what is freely given to us from God? Ten years had passed, and Sarah had not conceived from her husband. Is it possible that God freely gave her many years to enjoy her spouse without distraction? I do understand the longing for a child, but we must wait on him to visit our womb in his time.

1 To everything there is a SEASON, and a TIME to every purpose under the heaven:

2 A time to be born, and a time to die; a TIME to plant, and a TIME to pluck up that which is planted;

3 A TIME to kill, and a TIME to heal; a TIME to break down, and a time to BUILD up;

4 A time to weep, and a time to laugh; a time to mourn, and a time to dance;

5 A time to cast away stones, and a time to gather stones together; a time to embrace, and a time to refrain from embracing;

6 A TIME to get, and a time to lose; a time to keep, and a time to cast away;

7 A time to rend, and a time to sew; a time to keep silence, and a time to speak;

8 A time to love, and a time to hate; a time of war, and a time of peace.

9 What profit hath he that worketh in that wherein he laboureth?

10 I have seen the travail, which God hath given to the sons of men to be exercised in it.

11 He hath made everything beautiful in his time: also, he hath set the world in their heart, so that no man can find out the work that God maketh from beginning to the end.

Ecclesiastes 3:1-11

There is a song that says," He may not come when you want Him, but He will be there right on time, He's an on-time God yes He is." Speaking of singing let the body of Christ receive encouragement from Hannah's song and prayer.

1 And Hannah prayed, and said, my heart rejoiceth in the LORD, mine horn is exalted in the LORD: my mouth is enlarged over mine enemies; because I rejoice in thy salvation.

2 There is none holy as the LORD: for there is none beside thee: neither is there any rock like our God.

3 **Talk no more so exceeding proudly**; **let not arrogancy come out of your mouth**: for the LORD is a God of knowledge, and **by him actions are weighed**.

4 The bows of the mighty men are broken, and they that stumbled are girded with strength.

5 They that were full have hired out themselves for bread; and they that were hungry ceased: so that **the barren hath born seven**; and **she that hath many children is waxed feeble**.

6 **The LORD killeth**, and **maketh alive**: he bringeth down to the grave, and bringeth up.

{I Samuel 2:2-6}

Hannah had so much joy about being fruitful she sung unto the Lord. She said, "**Talk no more exceeding proudly**." Is it not speaking exceeding proudly when we boldly declare, "I'm not having all those children?" "I want to finish school first." "I want a boy and a girl, and that's it." There are so many more proud statements declared, worldwide, by women of God who have become "captains' of their own vessels," or should I say "**wombs**." Hannah also said, "**Let not arrogancy come out of your mouth**." Her womb received a visitation from the Lord, and it seems as if Hannah was prophesying to the women in our time. In more than one place in the Bible, it is recorded that God gives life.

Nevertheless, many continue to speak **arrogantly** against being fruitful and bringing forth life. Call a neighbor, call a friend; warn them saying, "refrain from speaking proudly and let not arrogance come out of your mouth."

All the above-mentioned excuses and declarations are centered on **self,** but what does the Lord have to say about it? **I want! I want!** But, I say unto you, seek ye first the kingdom of God and his righteousness. Hannah stated so beautifully, "<u>**By God**</u> <u>actions are weighed</u>."

{Proverbs 16:2-6}

2 All the ways of a man are clean in his own eyes; but the LORD weigheth the spirits.

3 Commit thy works unto the LORD, and thy thoughts shall be established.

4 The LORD hath made all things for himself: yea, even the wicked for the day of evil.

5 Every one that is proud in heart is an abomination to the LORD: though hand join in hand, he shall not be unpunished.

6 By mercy and truth iniquity is purged: and by the fear of the LORD men depart from evil.

REMEMBER

*Remember God does things according to his pleasing.

*Remember God can cause the barren to have seven children.

*Remember God can cause the woman who has many to wax feeble.

*Remember God made all things for himself.

*Remember he even made the wicked for the day of evil.

*Remember if he made wicked for the day of evil, he certainly made our children for a reason.

*Remember everyone who is proud in heart is an abomination to the Lord.

*Remember Pride makes you plan your family, versus seeing it as being freely given to you from God.

*Remember by mercy and truth iniquity is purged. God is merciful, so let the truth concerning this matter cleanse and purge you from the iniquity of seed counting.

Psalms 34:11-19

[11] **Come, ye children, hearken unto me: I will teach you the fear of the LORD.**

[12] What man is he that desireth **life**, and loveth many days, that he may see good?

[13] Keep thy tongue from evil, and thy lips from speaking guile.

[14] Depart from evil, and do good; seek peace, and pursue it.

[15] The eyes of the LORD are upon the righteous, and his ears are open unto their cry.

[16] The face of the LORD is against them that do evil, to cut off the remembrance of them from the earth.

[17] **The righteous cry, and the LORD heareth, and delivereth them out of all their troubles.**

[18] The LORD is nigh unto them that are of a broken heart; and saveth such as be of a contrite spirit.

[19] **Many are the afflictions of the righteous: but the LORD delivereth him out of them all.**

MANY ARE THE
AFFLICTIONS OF
THE RIGHTEOUS

Blindly all over the world, women are trying to save their life from the responsibility of motherhood. That's troubling; because saving my own life; at the expense of forbidding life does not seem wise at all, but selfish.

Lady J

Many Are the Afflictions of The Righteous

Margaret Sanger's mother had several miscarriages. Margaret believed that all these pregnancies took a toll on her mother's health and contributed to her early death. I lost my tenth child February of 2014. I know this sounds blunt, but if that tragedy had brought me to my demise, "it is the Lord that giveth and the Lord that taketh away." "Many are the afflictions of the righteous: but the LORD delivereth him out of them all." {Ps. 39:19}

Furthermore, the Bible says, "She shall be saved in childbearing if she continues in the faith with holiness and sobriety." The Lord did just that. He saved me. So, not even fetal demise is an excuse to try and save your life at the expense of a life. Come on Now! "Whosoever shall seek to save his life shall lose it; and whosoever shall lose his life shall preserve it." {Luke 17:33}

Blindly, all over the world, even Christian women are trying to save their life from the responsibility of motherhood. That is troubling, because saving my own life; at the expense of forbidding life, does not seem wise at all, but selfish.

{Luke9:23-24}

23And he said to them all. "If any man will come after me, let him deny himself, and take up his cross daily, and follow me.

24 For whosoever will save his life shall lose it but whosoever will lose his life for my sake, the same shall save it."

To allow your womb to be free according to God's pleasing is a major self-denial. The Lord said, when we come after Him, we must deny ourselves. A woman being fruitful and willing to multiply is a perfect example of denying herself. She is literally taking up her cross. Birth control is used because women fear the cross or burdens that await in their future. If we learn to take up our cross daily as instructed, we can rest in the fact that "Jesus' burden is light, and His yoke is easy." It want be so worrisome when we do it daily. If He brings us to it, He will bring us through it.

If He gives us children, they have a purpose just like Jeremiah, John, and Jesus. What is a man's advantage, if he gains the whole world, and loses himself, or be cast away? How many women put off bearing children seeking worldly possession? When they are finally ready to conceive, they realize it does not work like that. "For whosoever shall be ashamed of me and of my words, of him shall the son of man be ashamed, when he shall come in his own glory, and in his Father's, and of the holy angels." Matthew 25:31

As much as Jesus honored His Father, we should know fully that He is an advocate of procreation. "Also, Pastor Barry Jones Sr. added, "Women today are trying to avoid the persecution that comes along with being fruitful and multiplying. They don't want to challenge societal norms and stand on God's word. For example, the average Christian woman would adamantly reject abortion; however, they commonly accept birth control which is society's acceptable method of abortion," he expressed

Someone may say, "How can you place birth control on the same level as abortion?" Look at it like this, God spoke concerning Jeremiah in Jeremiah 1:5, "Before I formed thee in the belly I knew thee;" and before thou camest forth out of the womb I sanctified thee." But the women today say, under the influence of their contraceptives, before you form in my belly I abort thee. Before you come forth out of my womb I forbid thee.

Dictionary.com defines abort, "to bring forth a fetus from the uterus before the fetus is viable; miscarry." Another definition is to fail, cease or stop at an early or premature stage. The last, describes the wrongful premature ceasing or prohibiting of a child according to God's standard, considering He declares life before being formed. If you do not believe that, then you don't believe in the very Christ who you call "Savior. The Bible declares in John 1:1-3, "In the beginning was the Word, and the Word was with God, and the Word was God. The same was in the beginning with God. All things were made by him; and without him was not anything made that was made. Verse fourteen continues, "The word was made flesh and dwelt among us, (and we beheld his glory as of the only begotten of the Father full of grace and truth." {John 1:1-3 v. 14}

Jesus existence was present before he physically dwelt among men. Isaiah prophesied of Christ's coming years before his birth. He said in Isaiah 7:13-14, "Hear ye now, O house of David; Is it a small thing for you to weary men, but will ye weary my God also? Therefore, the Lord himself shall give you a sign; Behold a virgin shall conceive, and bear a son, and shall call his name Immanuel." {Isaiah 7:13-14}

For unto us a child is born, unto us a son is given: and the government shall be upon his shoulder: and his name shall be called Wonderful, Counsellor, The mighty God, The Everlasting Father, The Prince of Peace.

{Isaiah 9:6}

I think it is important to ask ourselves, "Does birth control weary God? "The Bible clearly lists the genealogy of Christ. He passed through forty-two generations; to be born, to live, then die and rise again on the third day, just for you and me. Believe it or not our families have a genealogy as well, and the babies that are aborted and forbidden by us, still count. Malachi, the prophet whose writing is just before Matthew where the birth of Jesus is found, spoke of a messenger who would be sent. Malachi 3:1 read, *"He shall prepare the way before me: and the Lord, whom ye shall seek, shall suddenly come to his temple, even the messenger of the covenant, whom ye delight in: behold, he shall come, saith the Lord of Host."*

So, John was spoken of before his existence also. He later came forth and paved the way for the Lamb of God. You and I by the Grace of God are children of Abraham our forefather. We were in that number when God spoke back then, "saying Abraham will be the father of many nations." I know you remember the children's song, Father Abraham. It says, "Father Abraham had many sons, many sons had Father Abraham, I am one of them and so are you so let's just praise the Lord." Can we praise the Lord for the truth, because knowing it makes us free? *Even as Abraham believed God, and it was accounted to him for righteousness. Know ye therefore that they which are of faith, the same are the children of Abraham.*

{Galatians 3:6-7}

I remember when the scribes and Pharisees told Jesus, "We be Abraham's seed." They were upset because Jesus was telling them, "Ye shall know the truth, and the truth shall make you free." Jesus rebuked them sharply saying, "If ye were Abraham children, ye would do the works of Abraham." Abraham readily accepted his calling to father many nations before our existence. My Lord if he can accept fathering many nations, I know we can handle the amount numbered to us by God. Abraham was even concerned when he saw he had not produced offspring. The scribes and Pharisees were spiritually blind. Likewise, there is a measure of blindness concerning this topic presently. If God spoke of us before our existence, declaring that "Abraham would be father to many nations," who are we to dictate our wombs? Let's just Praise the Lord, right? We profess to be children of Abraham while forbidding our own children. It was his obedience that brought us here, and not just us, but Christ Himself. Jesus was spoken of and was accounted for years before his existence. Likewise, all of our children were surely accounted for before their existence.

THINE EYES DID SEE
MY SUBSTANCE

However, Sister Thompson had a dream there were fish in a tank, but one of the fishes was leaning over to the side. It had died!

Lady J

Thine Eyes Did See My Substance

Psalms 139:16

Somebody may still be a little doubtful about the fact that children are predestined. I submit a case in point...My Twins! Years before I had my twins the Lord revealed it to me repeatedly. Okay, just to name a few: **Sister Cynthia Donaldson** dreamed that she walked in the church and there were twins in two car seats on the pew. She went to admire the babies, and someone said, "Those are Sister LaShela twins." Then she woke up.

I had a dream I was taking an ultrasound and the tech in my dream said, with a weird expression, "I see a shadow." He got silent then said, "Mrs. Jones, you have two babies." I jumped clean off the table then I woke up. **My husband** had a dream that I was sitting on a bench with my back to him. There were girl-boy twins sitting with me; one on the right and one on the left. My friend **Threase Moye** had a dream that I had twins. It was a girl and a boy.

I said in the dream that I was naming the boy seven. She said, she asked me why seven, I did explain, but she did not remember the explanation. Well here is the interpretation. I had the twins after having seven children and the boy was born first. Wow! **Minister Jacqueline Williams** had at least three dreams, that I had twins. **Sister Michelle Brun** had a dream; I was sitting with two basinets. She said, "The colors led her to believe, that it was boy-girl twins." Minister Lataurus Glover dreamed she was helping my husband take two car seats to our van. What made her dream so weird is she told me her dream the next day after Michelle Brun told me hers. Minister Katina Johnson had a dream that I had twins. Sister Seretha Bass dreamed that I had twins, and that it was a girl and a boy. I can go on and on. My point is, God revealed this to several people including my husband and me over the course of years.

It has surely come to pass and it proves that they were predestined before their conception. It was a regular night, I was pregnant with what I assumed was my eighth child. Keep in mind that I had an ultrasound appointment two days away. I heard these words in my spirit "**If this is so why am I thus?**" I asked my husband, "Who in the Bible said if this is so why am I thus?" Pastor Jones said, "Rebekah, she was pregnant with twins."

I said, "Oh my goodness, I think the Lord is telling me I'm pregnant with twins!" My ultrasound proved just that! God revealed it to His people; he even spoke to me while I was carrying them, just days before the confirmation. Hallelujah! Many days prior to finding out I was carrying twins; I experienced severe nausea as never before. I can recall thinking, "What is wrong with me?" I knew it was not normal at all. The blessed day that I learned there were two babies, I understood Rebekah's statement, "If this is so why am I thus? Rebekah wanted to know what was going on inside of her. I wondered the same thing; my nausea seemed doubled just like my seed.

20 And Isaac was forty years old when he took Rebekah to wife, the daughter of Bethuel the Syrian of Padanaram, the sister to Laban the Syrian.

21 And Isaac intreated the LORD for his wife, because she was barren: and the LORD was intreated of him, and Rebekah his wife conceived.

22 And the children struggled together within her; and she said, If it be so, why am I thus? And she went to enquire of the LORD.

23 And the LORD said unto her, two nations are in thy womb, and two manner of people shall be separated from thy bowels; and the one people shall be stronger than the other people; and the elder shall serve the younger

24 And when her days to be delivered were fulfilled, behold, there were twins in her womb.

25 And the first came out red, all over like a hairy garment; and they called his name Esau.

26 And after that came his brother out, and his hand took hold on Esau's heel; and his name was called Jacob: and Isaac was threescore years old when she bare them.

{*Genesis 25:21-26*}

God is so good. His eyes saw our substance before it was complete. Just like God saw my twins before they were formed, he saw the conception and death of my tenth child before it was formed. **Prophetess Marion Collins** had a dream that Sister **Tamekia Thompson, another young lady,** and I were pregnant at the same time. It came to pass. All three of us were pregnant.

However, Sister Thompson had a dream that there were fish in a tank, but one of the fishes was leaning over to the side. It had died! Have you ever heard someone say, "I dreamed of fish, somebody is pregnant?"

God used something common (fish), to reveal that one of the babies was not going to make it. Unfortunately, it was my baby that passed away. Sister Thompson and I have been friends since we were young girls. She assumed it was her baby. She was grieved to find that it was mine. We cried together! I remember breaking down, as I heard her say so sweetly, "Lord not her child!" Both she and the other young lady had their babies, and they are doing just fine.

Prophetess Collins saw the conception of my child before it was formed. My baby was in the heart of God even though it did not make it. Think about that. That is very deep! She saw my pregnant belly before the child was conceived. Sister Thompson saw the death of the child before it came to pass. That proves the case of being predestine to me.

Being born is **predestined**. **Death** is also **appointed** as well. The bible says in Hebrews 9:27, *"And as it is appointed unto men once to die, but after this the judgment."*

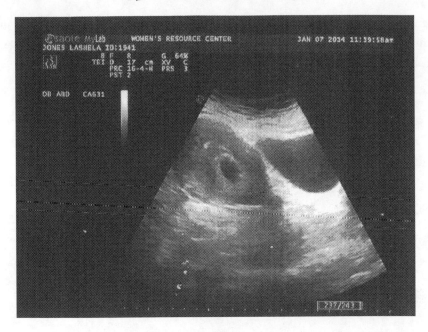

This ultrasound was taking on January 07, 2014; my child was still alive and active. On February 4, 2014 we learned of our child's demise. "**Rest in Peace my Child**" **Appointed** is defined as, predetermined; arranged; set. I know this child's **conception** and **demise** was predetermined, arranged, set, and appointed by God.

Losing my child is by far the hardest trial that I have ever faced. Not to mention, nearly losing my life in the process. I am so thankful God spared my life and gave me another chance to work while it is day. I am reminded of a story in the Bible. This story is personal because I know it could have been me. **BUT GOD**! Rachel proclaimed after her first son, "The Lord shall add to me another son." She seemed to be walking in foreknowledge. She saw in advance what was to come. Either that or she was speaking by **faith**. Her husband Jacob got up one day and said to his household, "Put away the strange gods that are among you. "He went on to say, "Be clean, and change your garments. I want to encourage someone, sometimes it seems like our hardest test comes when we are truly living a set aside life. Jacob was cleaning house, he was taking a stand for God. *Genesis 35:4 records," And they gave unto Jacob all the strange gods which were in their hand, and all their earrings which were in their ears; and Jacob hid them under the oak which was by Shechem."*

Afterwards, God appeared to Jacob again and blessed him. He even changed his name. He said, "Thy name is Jacob: thy name shall not be called any more Jacob, but Israel shall be thy name: and he called his name Israel." God told Jacob to be fruitful and multiply. I had to learn the hard way that even when you are sold out to being fruitful and multiplying death will still come. It is at those times when we must continue to trust the Lord, even the more. As Israel journeyed with his family, Rachel began to travail and have hard labor.

16 And they journeyed from Bethel; and there was but a little way to come to Ephrath: and Rachel travailed, and she had hard labour.

17 And it came to pass, when she was in hard labour, that the midwife said unto her, Fear not; thou shalt have this son also.

18 And it came to pass, as her soul was in departing, (for she died) that she called his name Benoni: but his father called him Benjamin.

19 And Rachel died, and was buried in the way to Ephrath, which is Bethlehem.

20 And Jacob set a pillar upon her grave: that is the pillar of Rachel's grave unto this day.

As you can see from the above verses, God did add to Rachel another son. However, she did not live to nurture it, nor did she have the privilege of raising him. Lord Have Mercy! We must watch our words. Rachel said, "give me children else I die." She died! That story shakes me, because many times I have been in travail and had hard labor. I knew each time that it was not normal pain. I also knew it was God alone who brought me on the other side of it alive.

Even in the face of death we must continue in obedience. I have just one question for death. O death, where is thy sting? O grave, where is thy victory?

Hallelujah!

{1Corinthians15:55}

TURN ON THE LIGHT

Infertility is a diagnosis that means you cannot get pregnant (conceive). If infertility means, there is a problem, or something is wrong. How can purposely making yourself infertile be right? I'm just asking.

Lady J

Turn on The Light!

Remember, it is the possible chance of becoming pregnant that influences birth control use. If you thought there was a possible chance of one of your loved ones being poisoned, would you do everything in your power to save their life? Of course, you would; and your actions would only be based on the possible chance of it happening.

Turn on the Light!

If you receive a call stating that a bomb was in the building you are in, would you leave? Of course, you would, because there is a possible chance of your life ending, right? It is a proven scientific fact that each human being's life begins at the point of conception. In sexual reproduction, that happens during the very first stage of fertilization. You have people who have a green thumb and are pros when it comes to fertilization of plants, flowers, and trees but refuse to let children fertilize and grow.

Turn on the Light!

Why is it that, if there is a possible chance at life being in jeopardy, it is worth saving? But the possible chance of life being born is optional to save?

Turn on the Light!

I remember when I was about to deliver my twins. The doctor literally screamed at me threatening to have me probated. Probated? Honey, I have never been to jail a day in my life. I certainly did not come this far to be probated. Especially, not on the Lord side. This rude and very disrespectful gesture was simply because I asked him, "to wait until my husband was present before he began." He was not even my doctor, so this was a stranger insulting my intelligence a little too early in the morning. His overreacting was because I was supposedly putting my life and the lives of my twins in danger. Keep in mind; he had only been aware of me being in labor for minutes. Not to mention, there was no sign of distress in the babies or me.

I'm not ignorant by a long shot. It was shift change and he was the on- call staff doctor. He had literally minutes before my doctor came on duty. His anger erupted from fear of losing thousands of dollars to the one who rightfully deserved it, my OB who took care of me the entire time. My point is, he was willing to have me probated due to a life supposedly being in danger. However, that same doctor will upon discharge offer me contraceptives to prevent life from coming forth. **REALLY?**

Turn on the Light!

Think about it! When someone has been murdered it is agreed that their life has been intentionally, prematurely terminated. Likewise, when contraceptives are in use we intentionally, and prematurely terminate. When that intended child comes down from God either it is going to "connect and grow or be hindered and go." Remember, birth control prevents the possible chance of life, right? Terminated: to end; an end to something: to bound or limit; especially: a distal end of an anatomical part.

Turn on the Light

How can we, with our mouth admit that birth control is to keep life from coming forth, but with the same mouth say, "it is not taking a life?" Infertility is a diagnosis that means you cannot get pregnant (conceive). If Infertility means, there is a problem, or something is wrong, how can purposely making yourself infertile be right? The disabling that birth control provides brings assurance to one, while that same disabling is a medical horror for another. How can this be right? How can it be a medical condition for one, while another freely intentionally inflict the symptoms of the medical condition upon themselves? How can one have joy in what brings sorrow to another?

Turn on the Light!

The Pill prevents ovulation. It obstructs sperm from reaching the oocyte (prevent fertilization) by thickening the cervical mucus. If the human has been created, contraceptives prevent implantation in the mother's womb. This is caused by the thinning of the lining of the uterus, resulting in the death of the child. This process is known as chemical abortion.

Turn on the Light!

If life is what you are trying to prevent, is that not a life prevented? Birth control only became legal in 1965, a year before my husband's birth. We must be **careful** when embracing everything that the natural law deems lawful. We should be very sure it does not break <u>the law of God</u>. There are ways to **defy** the <u>law of gravity</u> with positive results, such as flying a plane. However, there are seldom any positive results to defying <u>the law of God</u>!

Turn on the Light

The law should not override the Word of God or what has been established by the founding fathers. The law gives a woman the right to take birth control, but is it right in the sight of God? Contraceptives may be able to stop the sperm from connecting to an egg but does not stop nor change the fact that the Lord brought you an inheritance, but you declined.

<u>When is it</u> <u>okay to decline anything from the Lord</u>? Remember, every good and perfect gift comes from above. Let's just say the sperm connected but the contraceptive blocked it and prevented implantation. **<u>The Lord still</u> <u>came to visit you, right</u>**? Maybe the kind you use prevents the release of an egg. Your son or daughter is still dashed against the wall of your choice of contraceptive. I can cry when I think of many women who are taking contraceptives in vain. The Lord has already given them all the children He intended, what a shame!

Turn on the Light! Out of fear of motherhood, they continue their routine to stop the possible chance of life. One egg leaves a woman's ovary and travels into her fallopian tube. On average, a man can release millions of sperm, but only one has to swim up to meet her egg in order to make a "homerun," or should I say make a baby? Before life comes, we want to control it and keep it from coming. However, after life is here we go to all extremes to save it and keep it here.

Turn on the Light! How can putting a plastic **"bag"** over a child's head, be illegal, but wearing a condom is okay? Did you get that mental picture? Putting a possible life in that latex condom (**bag**) is acceptable but even if a child survives an intentional **"bag"** encounter, it will still be attempted murder at the least. People are charged and judged if they throw away their children or cause bodily harm. However, people engage in intercourse, release it in latex, chuck it away, and keep it moving until next time. I believe the blood of children is crying out to God! **<u>Lord Have Mercy!</u>** Making babies is for those who are married, and marriage is very serious. If one is not ready for all the responsibilities of marriage, it should not be taking lightly. Intimacy is only a fraction of the true purpose of marriage. If we look at marriage as just an opportunity to have sex, shame on us. Many want the pleasures of intimacy minus accountability, minus the responsibility of being fruitful.

A VERY IMPORTANT CHAPTER OF BEING FRUITFUL & MULTIPLYING

"It looks like your baby doesn't have a heartbeat,"
she said, nowhere near as sensitive as she could
have. She went on to explain that the baby was
twelve weeks measuring at seven weeks.

Lady J

A Very Important Chapter of Being Fruitful and Multiplying

Imagine losing all your children in one day. I cannot fathom such a tragedy. My afflictions, though horrific, seem light in comparison to Job's. Take a glimpse of the final minutes leading up to him discovering all ten of his children died in one day:

18 While he was yet speaking, there came also another, and said, thy sons and thy daughters were eating and drinking wine in their eldest brother's house:

19 And, behold, there came a great wind from the wilderness, and smote the four corners of the house, and it fell upon the young men, and they are dead; and I only am escaped alone to tell thee.

20 Then Job arose, and rent his mantle, and shaved his head, and fell down upon the ground, and worshipped,

21 And said, Naked came I out of my mother's womb, and naked shall I return thither: The LORD gave, and the LORD hath taken away; blessed be the name of the LORD.

22 In all this Job sinned not, nor charged God foolishly.

{Job 1:18-22}

I must say the above verses sustained me in a very difficult time in my life. Job had just received the horrible news that all ten of his children died in one day. Monday night we went to bed on cloud nine. Can you believe it? Our very first television broadcast aired that night! We were delighted to be interviewed. One of the topics of discussion was about being fruitful and multiplying. We were able to discuss our views on the importance of letting God number our seed. Tuesday morning started as a great day. We were excited because I had a prenatal appointment. This appointment was important because we were getting the results of some prior test take.

Yes! The test results were good! We tried to hear the baby's heartbeat, but there was nothing. My midwife assured me that it was not a big deal. "You are still early," she says. She decided to send us to get an ultrasound. I tell you I looked at that screen so eagerly, searching for my baby's activity.

Unfortunately, assuming I was too early to really see anything, I could not discern that there was no heartbeat at all. I am still clueless at this point hearing the tech say, "she had to do a vaginal ultrasound because she could not find a heartbeat." No big deal, "I am still early I convinced myself." I was so happy for myself and excited for this baby, which even after the tech left for the doctor, I still just did not get it. My husband looked at me with a serious face and said, "I have looked at these screens many times and there is literally no heart beat."

I was shocked to silence while my worse prenatal fear was consuming me at a fast pace. Meanwhile, the doctor returned and searched diligently for a heartbeat that she never found. "It looks like your baby does not have a heartbeat," she said, nowhere near as sensitive as she could have. She went on to explain that the child was twelve weeks measuring at seven weeks. "Excuse me", I'm thinking, "She must be in the wrong room." After asking her softly several times, "So you think the baby is gone?" She responded, "Yes" each time. I knew then she was in the right room. I am not in a nightmare, I am being told my child was deceased and had been for a little while. "Are you Serious Satan?" I thought. "Are you trying to mock me?" Just that quick the enemy expressed to me, "Your voice went across the airwaves last night and your baby is dead."

How can this happen to me? I am proclaiming the good news about being fruitful and my child dies? This is the devil himself. Even in our vulnerable moments, pride will step in and make us think we do not deserve what we are going through. God gave his only Son for me, but I felt like I was given a raw deal. That was an indirect way of questioning God, versus accepting what He allows. "The devil is mocking me", "I shouted, crying and weeping sore.

It was an outburst of anguish and pain, you know, like Job's wife. She said, "You still maintain thy integrity, curse God and die." Have you ever heard that she was foolish for making such a statement? Did anybody consider how it feels to have ten children pass away in one day, and your husband is sick?

My husband took a stand against the enemy. He began to console me and correct me all at once. He said, "The devil is not in this," be encouraged, this is a very important chapter in being fruitful and multiplying." Whoa! It was as if everything stood still. I knew it was my husband's voice, but God was speaking through him to me. Just like Eli's words calmed Hannah, I became calm enough to realize that as the scripture promised, God saved me in childbearing. Important chapter! Ding! Ding! Ding! "Remember, LaShela, you are writing a book! Conception and Childbirth, right?"

That experience and all the pain it entails is an added chapter. It really is. Fetal demise is a part of conception. It is a part of being fruitful and multiplying as well. One of my favorite scriptures that have helped me through many prenatal challenges has just come alive and has taken on a brand-new meaning. I have been through a lot prenatally, but never fetal demise. How could I speak so confidently, if I had not experienced such pain? "Notwithstanding, she shall be saved in childbearing, if she continues in the faith and charity and holiness with sobriety.

I Timothy 2:15

Childbearing is the act or process of carrying and giving birth to a child. I am thankful for a mind to be saved and a heart to repent quickly; if that were not the case my situation may not have been so successful. I walked around for weeks with my child dead inside of me, having no clue. I know it is God's grace and mercy that kept me.

"Want He Do It?"

or should I say…

Didn't He do it!!!

Heritage- A special or individual possession; an allotted portion. Pregnancy is a reward from God Himself. Children are a heritage from the Lord. John 16:3

JOHN 16:21

After being rushed to the hospital via ambulance; I was appalled by how the staff was responding, considering my huge blood loss. I remember saying over and over "I'm bleeding like a faucet!" "I'm bleeding like a faucet!"

Lady J

John 16:21

A woman when she is in travail has sorrow, because her hour has come: but as soon as she is delivered of the child, she remembers no more the anguish, for joy that a man is born into the world. I did not realize that day; I was going to need my favorite scripture less than a week later. Truly, what occurred next surpassed anything I have ever fathomed. I was instructed to go home and to return Tuesday, February 11, 2014, to have a D&C (Dilation and curettage). They explained that if I started to bleed heavily to come straight to the Emergency room. Monday night, I was at my desk doing some computer work. I was anticipating my procedure the next day. I would cry from time to time, just thinking about my child being inside of me deceased. The doctor did not send me to surgery as soon as we found out; because she wanted to give it a week to pass on it's on. My blood was light all day, no problems. I stood up and a big gush immediately began to flow from my body. Believe it or not, although shocked, I was still surprisingly calm.

I figured, "Okay, this is what they meant. This is my cue to go to the hospital." I must say, my calmness escaped quickly. While trying to clean up to go to the hospital, I bled profusely. I recall using an entire roll of tissue. I could not stand because the blood was flowing from me like a faucet. I remember sitting and my husband standing in front of me holding me up. His body was a leaning post for me. He being there was the only thing keeping me from hitting the floor. I started drifting in and out of consciousness, which made my husband realize that driving to the hospital, was not an option. "I uttered a couple of times, "I'm dying as my strength was leaving me quickly."

Testimonial

"I can remember that day clearly. It was just another typical day. My god-mother Lady Jones was sitting at the computer handling business; suddenly she rushed quickly to her restroom. From there, everything happened; even the more swiftly. She was passing so much blood that she began to faint in and out. My god-father Pastor Jones called 911; and helped me clean her up. I was helping while in shock at the same time. My god-father and I brought her to the living room where she was later loaded onto a stretcher and taken to the hospital".

Sister Felicia Thomas

Jones Children's Testimonials

*My name is **Delvin D'Juan Jones**. I am a 16-year-old in the tenth grade. I am thankful to be the first child of nine siblings. I am a Holy Ghost filled musician in training (God being my teacher). My parents are Pastor Barry Jones and Elect-Lady LaShela Jones. I remember the day my world stood still. We were all excited when we were told another child was added to my parent's marvelous, fun-filled collection of nine children. A couple of months later I was having a strenuous day. Nothing seemed to feel right. I even had a rough day with home-school. When my mom walked in, she said nothing welcoming. She broke down the news to us kids, she said, "our baby passed away." My mind screamed but I dared not to cry. However, the more I tried to hold it in; the pressure began to build up inside of me. As tears began to roll down my face I could not talk, and I felt like I could barely breathe. Shortly after the hurt of the baby had been lifted, all seemed to be good for the family. Momma was at the computer working and I was folding cloths at the dinner table. Suddenly, she let out a slight gasp and I heard the sound of something dripping. Mom rushed to the bathroom. When I turned around I saw a trail of red from where she had been sitting, I realized it was blood. My dad came to my mom's aide, he asked me to help hold the children back. I remember trying to hold my brother back; he wanted so badly to check on momma. As he asked what was wrong, my words seemed to choke me. I didn't want to face the truth of what was really going on. When the ambulance wheeled away with mamma in the back, I could only hope that she would live. After she came back the worries was over. I am so glad momma was spared as well as saved in childbearing. Therefore, I am a firm believer in letting God number your seed. Families should not put God in a quote on quote cage. From my standpoint I think God used my baby sibling's death, and Momma's escape from death's door, as my wake-up call to follow him even the closer than I had been doing. **Delvin***

*My name is **Barry D. Jones Jr**. I am twelve years old and the second child of nine. I have been saved since age eight. I am thankful for my parents Pastor Barry D. Jones Sr., and Elect-Lady LaShela Jones. I remember watching a TV show called nineteen kids and counting. The episode was when their twentieth child died. My siblings and I was watching the show very closely. After the show I thought, I hope that never happen to us, my second thought was it will not happen because it never happened before. Not long after that my mom and dad gathered all the children in the living room. My mom was rolling tears and my dad had a very serious look on his face. I knew something was wrong. My mom said that the tenth baby died. All of us were rolling tears. I could not speak much for the rest of the day; I was very, very, shocked. Shortly after, it was a good day. Later that day there was a big problem, I was asked to leave the kitchen. I did not know what was going on, I wanted to see, but I had to stay in my room.*

I wanted to know what was wrong with my mom. I know that my mom had to go to the hospital. The ambulance was at my house, and I saw my mom on the stretcher. My eyes were filled with tears. That night I could not go to sleep. I found out a couple of days later she was ok, that's why it's good to be saved and to be fruitful and multiply. **Barry**

*Hello, my name is **Zachery Joel Jones**. I am the third child of nine. I am ten years old, and I am saved. I can remember the first idea that came to my mind, when I heard my mom was having a baby. "It's going to be a boy!" My thoughts were with joy, because I promised to never speak negative about babies again. I'm not going there with that story. I love the thought of birth, especially because I enjoy having a lot of brothers and sisters. When mom pulled us in to talk, I was happy for what she was about to say, until she said it. In tears of course, she said, "Your father and I found out the baby passed away." I instantly began to cry. A little later after that I was on my way up front, but my siblings said I could not go. I wondered, "What is going on." Then out of the window I saw the ambulance. When I heard that I was not able to say goodbye, I was in tears. I ran to my mom room only to find that she was gone. I wept. Three days later I heard that she was okay, I was thanking God for saving my mom.* **Zachery**

*My name is **Hannah D'Lois Jones**. I am the fourth child of nine children. I am nine years old; I got saved at age seven. When I first learned that my mom was pregnant, it came to me that something bad was going to happen to the baby. A few months later my mom and dad called us all in the living room. Everything seemed to be filled with joy, but when I saw my parents face, I already knew it was something about the baby. One night I was in my room and something was going on. Mom was in the ambulance. About three days later, mom was on her way home. I was watching and looking out the window until the car pulled up. When I saw the car, I rushed out the door and gave mom a big hug. I carried her things inside. When she sat on the couch I knew she was not all the way healed, but she was ok. Since I have been saved, I got up every morning to pray and read my bible. After what happened to mom, I stopped reading and praying for about a month. But today I am striving to stay on track.* **Hannah**

After being rushed to the hospital via ambulance; I was appalled by how the staff was responding, considering my huge blood loss. I remember saying over and over **"I'm bleeding like a faucet!" "I'm bleeding like a faucet!"** Shockingly, my nurse asked me to walk to the bathroom to get a urine sample. The contractions were so painful, but what added to the pain is, it was not going to result in my child going home with me. The reality of my child's death was stinging like a bee.

This was all new. Even though my blood loss was extremely frightening to me; I assumed this was the normal process of a miscarriage. I constantly fought off with prayer the thoughts that I was gradually declining. Imagine sitting in a hospital bed, from my hips down to my calf was a pool of blood. I used the word "pool" because usually something wet, will absorb through a sheet. My blood "pooled" on the bed! No one seemed alarmed by it but my husband and me. That led me to believe, again, "this was normal for a miscarriage." However, I knew my blood loss was not normal at all. My gut feeling confirmed that to me without having anything to compare it to.

I was extremely week and feeling faint. Three doctors, nurses and a midwife were in my presence that night, and not one of them discerned that I was hemorrhaging. I did not know what to think of my declining health. The staff was very relaxed, while blood poured out of me, "**BLOOP, BLOOP, BLOOP.**" No lie! I could hear the blood pooling out. I felt I should have gone immediately into surgery, or at least they would stabilize my blood loss. While my second ultrasound was being performed, I began to feel extremely hot.

"I feel like I'm about to pass out," I told the tech. She started to fan me and bam, I passed out. After regaining my consciousness, I recall hearing that my blood pressure was seventy-something over thirty-something. "My goodness what was it before that?" "I wanted my God, I wanted my husband who was not allowed to come with me and had no idea what I was experiencing." Guess what? Everything went <u>rush</u>, <u>rush</u>, <u>rush</u>. I remember the ER nurse robbing my arm. She looked so afraid. I think she realized that she did not respond properly to the emergency. Finally, I was taken to surgery. I heard the doctor tell my husband earlier that my female organs may have to be removed depending on what was found. You are going to think I'm crazy. As soon as I came from under anesthesia I said, "<u>**Are my female organs still in**</u>?"

Please allow me to laugh out loud (lol). I was very serious though! Even after something so horrific, I wanted to be obedient until death. After that experience, the average person would have welcomed removal of anything associated with conceiving a child. But I know my Redeemer lives. As I said earlier, "If he brings us to it he will bring us through it." While in the hospital room I was resting and recovering.

I can truly say I was relieved that I could finally start to heal physically, emotionally, mentally and spiritually. At least that is what I thought. My healing process was going to be delayed just a little longer. The first night was beautiful, "Can you believe it; a saved, sanctified, and Holy Ghost-filled woman of God was my nurse." We had a time in the Lord! I was the one in a mess, yet the Lord used me to encourage her.

She had several children like me but was very weary in well doing. The next day, I woke up feeling horrible. I could barely move. My limbs were stiff, and my face was stiff as well. I was extremely weak, and not myself at all. As I laid there feeling nearly lifeless, my husband and I assumed this was a part of the recovery process. Yet again, I had nothing to compare it to. In comes my chipper nurse, "Okay, time to take out your IV. You are discharging today. "My husband asserted himself and said, "Ma'am my wife is not leaving here until her blood is checked."

All I can say is his nearly thirty years of nursing experience came up and out of him. He started expressing some blood terminology that was way over my head. I am blessed to be married to a registered nurse huh? What he said caused the nurse to get the doctor. Both not knowing he was a nurse, felt he was clueless, and saw no need to check my blood again. "How do **you** feel," she said to me, as if to say your wife is the patient. When my blood came back they came hurling in, "**She needs a blood transfusion**," "**She needs a blood transfusion**!" Thank God for my husband's sensitivity. Thank God for his discernment!

I can only imagine what my situation would have come to, had I been discharged. The blood was running under my skin, instead of in my vein. **Scary!!** My arm was bruised for several weeks. I can truly say the life of the flesh is in the blood. After the blood transfusion I felt a whole lot better. **Meanwhile, a couple days later I was on my way home, I was stiff as a board from my face down.** I could only raise my arms so high. My recovery at home was bitter sweet. Finally, I could see my children. They were hurt when they learned we lost the baby. However, they were very happy to see me come home but, of course, not under those circumstances. God touched me daily and strengthened me in my inward man as well my physical body. I know people were praying for me.

One morning without restraints, I jumped out of the bed so quickly. Hallelujah, that stiffness was gone. The Lord took it away while I slept. No more walking like a robot!

A friend of mine who was living with me at the time, filled me in one day after I discharged from the hospital. "She said, "I can vividly recall that dreadful day... everything was normal until evening time. As you sat typing at the computer, you stood up and ran to the bathroom, leaving behind a trail of pooled blood. Not wanting to traumatize the children, I escorted them to their room, so I can clean up, while you were being attended to by your goddaughter and your husband. I went and reassured the children that everything was okay. As I came back up to the kitchen they were bringing you up from the back of the house (almost dragging you) you were very unstable do to blood loss. They laid you on your back on the floor in the living room and all I could think was "help Lord". As they waited for the ambulance to arrive there was growing concern among your children. Again, all I could do was reassure them everything was going to be alright. As I watched them take you out of the house all I could do was pray... I knew you were in God's Hands now." Everything happened so fast I can only imagine, how that sight looked to all present. It was very scary for me.

We were asked, "Are you skeptical now?" My final answer is, "I do not feel in any way skeptical, I have come too far from where I started from."

Nobody told me the road would be easy. He did not bring me this far to leave me." I still don't have a mind to take contraceptives. I stand even the more firmly on my stance of being fruitful and multiplying. I had a total of nine children. From my first child to the ninth, many things have transpired to provoke me to control birth. After all I have been through, I am not tempted.

I can truly say I am not enticed. Beginning with my **first** child, **Delvin**, almost twenty years ago; <u>**I was aspirating on my vomit**</u>. The nurse was right there in the room and had no clue. My beloved friend of over twenty years, <u>**Shanika Jackson**</u>, was there at the time. She saw my distress, jumped on the bed and rolled me over. Vomit spewed all over the place. I don't remember her getting in the bed, nor do I remember her rolling me over. I do remember vomit shooting across the room.

That is scary simply because it reveals that I was only conscious long enough to vomit, in other words I was in a crisis. The anesthesia was administered at such a high dosage that it became like poison to my body.

Testimonial

*"This is my traumatic experience of witnessing my best friend's birth of her first born. Her mother, sister and I were in the room with her throughout this process. We were all excited, awaiting the arrival of her new bundle of joy. The nurse came into the room to check the progress of labor; I noticed that Lady J stopped talking while the nurse was speaking to the family. I said something is wrong, but the nurse replied and said, "She's just resting for the big moment. **She was just lying there with this blank stare and no movement**." I was not sure what was happening, but I just felt something was wrong. I jumped into the bed and sat across her stomach while rolling her to the side. As she rolled vomit shot across the room like on the movies. **She took this deep breath once her airway was free. I burst into tears as the nurse rushed to her aid**. We later realized **she was aspirating on her vomit**. Thank God for using me to save her."*

Sister Shanika Jackson

Just like Sister Nikki Jackson burst into tears, when I received her testimonial for this book I burst into tears as well. That was my first encounter with the other side of my birth story. I was touched when I learn that from the beginning, tragic seemed to gravitate to me during childbirth. But God!! The details of the story were lost in oblivion. It doesn't surprise me that Nikki just finished nursing school. Congrats baby! You were my nurse first friend; years before nursing ever crossed your mind. You are going to be a Terrific Nurse.

Unfortunately, as I said, I do not recall the particulars about that incident. Just prior things were progressing slowly; the (labor was thirty-six hours) but nothing abnormal. Only after receiving the epidural did things begin to decline. After speaking to my oldest sister, Helen and my Mother Delores, they confirmed that I also had a seizure immediately after aspirating.

My Mother went on to explain that the epidural given was too strong and I was not able to move myself. "They gave you too much of that medicine." "When you vomited it was green," Mama stated." This tragedy began because I was oblivious about choosing to birth His way. Finally, mama said, "You had two contractions and he was here."

My bundle of joy ended up with a shaved head to accommodate an IV and seven days in the hospital; therefore, I went home alone. With my second child, Barry, I was rushed to the hospital contracting majorly. I was six centimeters when I got there. I was so anxious about the pain, I begged for the epidural. I wish I knew then what I know now. Oh, how I wish I had someone to tell me, "calm down sister and take one contraction at a time." The anesthesiologist juiced me up good. I was so numb I could not feel my lower extremities.

This caused my son's heart rate to drop, forcing me into emergency surgery. He coded. I became very depressed about the outcome of that birth experience. I remember laying there during surgery. I was shaking so badly. It felt like I was about to have another seizure. I asked the anesthesiologist, "Why am I shaking like this? "He gave me a serious and nasty look, humped his shoulders and never uttered a peep. Tears dropped out of my eyes as sadness flooded my soul.

I did not regain feelings in my lower body until three days later. I cried and cried that hospital stay, as my birth story played back to me like a movie. God began to minister to my spirit that even though this was only my second child, **I was not doing birth His way**. I was so embarrassed, as I saw the re-run of my anxiousness for the epidural.

I sent them a couple of times to fetch the anesthesiologist, which was very irritating to him. It caused him to inject the medicine according to my anxiousness. So therefore, he knew good and well why I was shaking so badly. Here I am revisiting my first birth; again, I had too much of the epidural. Now I see why the Bible says, "Be careful for nothing; but in everything by prayer and supplication with thanksgiving let your request be made known unto God." {Philippians 4:6}

Unfortunately, this time I literally begged for a nightmare unawares. That birth experience grieved me for a while, simply because I knew my prenatal nightmares had just begun. This was a result of desperately wanting freedom from pain. Meanwhile I chose to stop crying about it and started studying about it. My studies revealed that pregnancy and birth is not a sickness and should not be treated as such. I realized pain was a necessary part of childbirth.

It's amazing how the main sign (pain) that reveals to us that our babies are coming forth, seems to be the first thing that we want to stop once it begins. Our flesh is really a mess!

If a full-term pregnant woman never starts to contract that would be an indication that something is wrong. Doctors look for the pain spoken from God to confirm the time of delivery. Yet they suggest pain meds when it arrives as if it is a pain from injury versus destiny. As for Christian women it should be taught that pain associated with birth is referenced in the Holy Scriptures. It is not ordinary pain, but purpose driven pain. Christian women should be taught good things, so as not to give occasion to the adversary. The same adversary from the beginning, who helped bring pain to childbirth; is turning our hearts from the consequences spoken from God.

And the LORD God said unto the woman, what is this that thou hast done? And the woman said, the serpent beguiled me, and I did eat.

And the LORD God said unto the serpent, Because thou hast done this, thou art cursed above all cattle, and above every beast of the field; upon thy belly shalt thou go, and dust shalt thou eat all the days of thy life:

And I will put enmity between thee and the woman, and between thy seed and her seed; it shall bruise thy head, and thou shalt bruise his heel.

Unto the woman he said, I will greatly multiply thy sorrow and thy conception; in sorrow thou shalt bring forth children; and thy desire shall be to thy husband, and he shall rule over thee. {Genesis 3:13-16}

Married women I advise you to grab hold to the desire for your husband, bare down and push! **Bring forth and bring forth <u>Christ's way</u>**! Everything that God says, the enemy will counter it with a rebuttal causing you to justify your compromise. Pain is a part of the normality of childbirth. The enemy's plot is to stop fruitfulness. He wants us to think it is okay to intentionally stop a God ordained process, which is painful. The scripture even encourages us saying, "Through much tribulation, we will enter into the kingdom of God." We cannot get around suffering for Christ. Likewise, we should not deviate from his written oracles concerning pain associated with childbirth.

One of my favorite scriptures says," But the God of all grace, who hath called us unto his eternal glory by Christ Jesus, after that ye have suffered a while, make you perfect, stablish, strengthen, settle you."

{1 Peter 5:10}

The birth of my **third** child, **Zachery,** was not tragic, however, I allowed a doctor to intimidate me. He forced a repeated c- section on me even after being nine centimeters dilated when I arrived at the hospital. I am sure you can see now why I said, my prenatal nightmares had just begun. The anesthesiologist made several attempts to put the epidural in my back. It was as if the Lord was blocking it, so that I could speak up.

(Remember Prophetess Collins Testimony)

I submitted to his position, causing a vicious cycle and an indictment on my future pregnancies. What do you mean one might ask? The rule of thumb seems to be, once you go c-section you don't go back. Anticipating my **fourth** child **Hannah**, I was so excited! Finally, I was having a girl after having three boys in row. This experience ended well but began with an extremely rude doctor who insisted that if he were going to be my doctor, I was having a c-section. He said to do otherwise was stupid. Suffice it to say, he was not my doctor much longer after that. I went all the way to Pascagoula, Mississippi to find a Physician. The doctors I spoke to in Mobile, said vaginal birth was not an option. Thankfully, I found a very sweet obstetrician there. I explained to my new OB, with tears, the reason why I had the previous c- sections.

He agreed saying, "because they were not due to a physical problem, he would allow me to have a v-bac. However, I had to agree to being scheduled, having the epidural, and fetal head monitoring. I tell you, **I was trying to climb my way up to the top of childbirth, His way**. I wanted zero interventions. I mean Zero! I was constantly met with opposition. It seemed to be one thing after another. I wanted no part of medical interventions. You must remember, this was my fourth child. I had known about birth Christ's way since my second child. However, the other side was I begged for this out of ignorance. Remember that second birth? I pleaded for an epidural; not realizing it would travel and torment me in my future pregnancies. Honey, I had no clue there would be future pregnancies.

Nevertheless, I really had to acknowledge the error of my ways. I had to admit that I could no longer walk in darkness concerning childbirth His way.

So here I am, not totally free to walk out my convictions, but I had the information I needed to stop the indictment. I am also trying to convey a point to you. Some Spur of the moment decisions can affect or lives for years to come. I decided, come what may, I was going all the way.

I had no idea I would multiply seven more times. However, I was ready for whatever I would go through. I did receive the epidural, but just like I begged for it with my second child, I begged him to stop it with this fourth child. Guess what? God gave me my heart's desire! He stopped it. I delivered natural! Yes! That little girl came so fast. "We did not have time to get dressed," exclaimed my nurse with joy. I felt so good. Yes Lord, I want childbirth your way! My fifth child Marion, you already know I am not hearing epidural, c-section, or any such like. I went back to the doctor who did the unnecessary c-section with baby number three. Apart from that indiscretion he was a good doctor. I told him with tears how I felt about being nine centimeters and getting cut. He felt bad and agreed to leave me alone and let my body do what it was inclined to do. Unfortunately, my labor stalled for hours. "This is so obvious," I thought. The hurdles are back again.

I had to weigh my options; which were a c-section (that was not a true option in my world), or the "PIT" (pitocin). "I'll take it, and that's it, no further," I said, feeling great irritation. My prenatal dukes were up, and I was sucker punching any intervention that would lead me off my v-bac path. The birth was beautiful. The pain from the PIT felt as it came from the Pit of H-E- double hockey sticks. Only God helped me to endure pitocin natural. That medicine they tell you will take the edge off the pain...They forgot to tell you it takes the wrong edge off. It only makes you super drunk then BANG, the contraction hits, knocking you out of your stupor.

We should be led when it comes to medicine, seeking God in all things. During this same pregnancy, I remember so well I had noonday prayer. Honey, I had a time! I went straight to the doctor, adrenalin flowing, and what is the first thing they do when you get to the doctor?

"They take your blood pressure." My pressure was super high. My doctor prescribed me B/P medicine after one high reading. For some reason I did not feel led to take it. Every appointment he would say "looks like we have you on the right meds for your pressure." All I could think is, "Thank God Jesus is my doctor."

By now, no one in their right mind would continue having children. Rest assured; I am very much in THE right mind, the mind of Christ. Hello world. I am pregnant again with number six, Temperance. By this time, I had studied and had become a certified doula (woman servant) with DONA International. I also became a Christian childbirth educator. My pregnancy was great! Another girl! I had three boys in a row, and now three girls in a row.

I remember so clearly baby Hannah walking up to me before church saying, "Mama, that baby still in your stomach?" No lie! I started contracting minutes later. Did this little girl prophesy, or at the least discern what was to come? I assured my husband (Pastor Jones) that I would be okay through service that night. We agreed to go to the hospital later. At this point, my husband had stepped out on faith and began his ministry. The church was approximately 2 1/2 years old. That night at church my contraction pattern was perfect. So, I thought, "Looks like Miss Temperance Louella is coming tonight."

I stepped into the prayer line the minister immediately began speaking prophetically, saying, "I see angels in your hospital room." She said, "God has given his angels charge over you." She spoke many other words that I so desperately needed later. I had no idea God was using her words to prepare me for what was to come. This time around, I hired a doula because I was finally free from the yokes of prenatal intervention. We labored together at home for hours. When I arrived at the hospital, I was seven centimeters dilated. "Yes!" "I have three more to go!" "This is a piece of cake." "I will be done in no time." That is what I thought. Wrong again! I made it to eight centimeters quickly and went no further.

My doula, my husband and I were so excited. Our excitement left after a couple of hours. "What's wrong?" I was still at eight centimeters hours later. One, two, three, four, five, six, seven, eight hours later, and I am still eight centimeters!

It was horrible. The pain was like nothing I had ever encountered. Each contraction felt like my insides were ripping apart. I cried and even asked for death. My midwife came in and said, "I cannot wait any further.

You must go back to surgery." I was so grieved, a midwife, doula, natural, and still no baby. I even had another midwife come to assist, when she learned my labor stalled. Without thinking, I jumped off the table. I had nurses on both sides trying to prep me for surgery. After jumping from their grips I shouted literally, "I'm mad at Satan." "I rebuke him in the name of Jesus," I proclaimed boldly.

I began to command Satan to let my child go free. I quickly squatted down, pushing with all my might. I had no idea what everybody else was doing. However, in hindsight, I imagine they thought I was crazy. I walked the floor, speaking in tongues, waiting eagerly for the next contraction, as if to say, "Hit me with your best shot." My second contraction I pushed hard three times. Temperance came forth with the cord wrapped tightly around her neck three times.

That is what held her up, hours upon hours. It was Jesus who brought my horror to shouts of joy and Hallelujah. It was as if He extended her cord just enough to come out. The room was filled with amazement, expressions of joy, laughter and plain astonishment. One of my nurses said, "I knew something was about to happen." "I could not get that IV in for nothing." Of course, that confirmed what I felt about God giving me a chance to speak up during Zachery's birth. I can truly say I would not wish the pain from that birth on an enemy. God is so faithful! My midwife was so amazed at how God stepped in for me. She insisted that my husband and I meet her dad, who was a pastor. Shockingly, her father, after meeting us once; asked us to pray about sharing the church building he was in.

We prayed, and God lead us to do so. We were privileged to abide there nine years. with unmerited favor. My pain brought us favor! How odd is that? I love Manna Ministries Inc. After that birth I preached a powerful message inspired by God; entitled PUSH, an acronym for Pray Until Something Happens.

Always remember prayer changes things. Two years later, I became pregnant again with my seventh child, Nathan. Call me crazy, but after my horrible time with Temperance I opted to do a home birth this time around. Honey let me tell you, a toothache and contractions at the same time is a horrific combo. Isn't that the truth Prophetess Collins? Wink! Wink! I called and begged my dentist to pull my tooth and not let me suffer with both types of pain. To my surprise, he did. Let the fun begin! It was so beautiful, I dilated quickly. My water even broke on its own this time, something I had never experienced. I ordered all my babies t-shirts saying, "I'm a big brother/sister." I got to ten centimeters quickly and stayed there even longer than I remained at eight centimeters the previous pregnancy. I ended up taking a trip to the hospital.

"I just cannot believe this," I am here again. How can someone who is set on doing right be faced with what seems to go wrong constantly. Some may feel I was totally overboard in what I tolerated. My midwife, who was a blessing to me the previous pregnancy, this time around became weary with me. My baby just would not come down. Two obvious choices were there, get an epidural and pitocin to push the baby down, or the "C" word (c- section). My midwife refused to let me get the epidural and try to push. That hurt me so bad because I had to get it anyway to have a c-section. If I had to choose between a major surgery and an epidural, it would be the epidural. Medical intervention was necessary and welcomed. I would have been selfish if I did not consider her feelings. She knew of my history, and patiently supported me through prenatal trials that seemed to get worse each pregnancy. At that point, I successfully had three vaginal births after c-sections. Unfortunately, I spiraled backwards, she sent me to surgery.

"Lord, I just had my seventh child. No one will listen to me for sure now." My midwife and I talked at my postpartum appointment, she apologized with tears. She admitted that the epidural should have been the first option not surgery. She also stated, "That was a lesson learned and I will hold it dear to my heart throughout the rest of my career." She knew that surgery was a stumbling block for me if I were to conceive again. I became ill after Nathan was born. I had a fever and my recovery even after being home, was very trying. It took a couple of weeks to bounce back. Mother Brenda Gill called to check on me. That woman of God prayed so hard on that phone.

She rebuked the spirit of infirmity off of me. Yes, it did flee and quickly too! I love me some Mother Gill. She helped take care of me during my hospital stay. She is just like my second mom. I honor her; along with my dear mothers at Manna Ministries, who love me and my family so sweetly.

Guess what friends, I am pregnant with twins. I was diagnosed with gestational diabetes and hypertension. On top of that, I was admitted to the hospital at 32 weeks because I had protein in my urine. I cried, as I packed my bags, preparing to stay in the hospital on bed rest until I delivered. The hospital stay that week was good. Manna Ministries was instrumental in keeping me encouraged. My husband and Juicy were champions.

They kept things at home flowing like a charm. I even had my baby shower in the hospital. The staff was so open to it and very sweet. Those sanctified women at Manna; I tell you they lit that place up with prayer. The janitor even came in and prophesied to me! I remember one Sunday morning Pastor J came to see me before he went to church. He stepped out the room and it took him a minute to come back. One of the staff members asked him to pray for them. They went down the hall, honey; she purged in a trash can. I was like, "Whoa, that's what I'm talking about. God is moving in here" Nevertheless, the question in the back of my mind was, "Wow" "Lord how long will I be here?"

The next week God stepped in. I started contracting and continued all night. I did not say a word, because I was so desperate to see what my body was going to do. My nurse asked me was I in pain. If ignoring was not rude, Lord knows, I would have done so. Lying was not an option. I knew what was going to happen when she learned I was contracting. When the nurse learned I was in labor, rush, rush, rush, again. "What is the big deal?" I have been this way all night. You read a portion of the story earlier.

To make a long story short, I had another C-section. My twins gave me a grand total of nine children they were born at 33 weeks. Nahum was 5lbs. 2oz. and Naomi was 4lbs. 4oz. They fared well and did not stay in NICU long. However, I thought I was going to hyperventilate when they cut Naomi's gray patch of her hair out.

(The gray patch is my family's birth mark). That is another story! Apart from the sadness of having a c-section everything else went well.

After all of this is said and done, it may seem ludicrous to have continued to multiply nine times and certainly after all those complications. I look at it differently.

I have a wide range of birth experiences, making it easy for me to relate to women. The details found in this book only scrape the surface of the actual stories. I believe even the more that being fruitful, and multiplying is the perfect will of God. There are no excuses. There is a way that seems right; but the end thereof is death." Let us give the most earnest heed to the things we have heard, lest at any time we should let them slip. My reasoning for why I do what I do, can be found in the following verse: A woman when she is in travail hath sorrow, because her hour is come: but as soon as she is delivered of the child, she remembereth no more the anguish, for joy that a man is born into the world.

{John 16:31}

Can I get a Witness?

Is it ok that we have one more witness from the scriptures? You know the story, Ruth followed her mother-n-law Naomi. When we honor and serve with a pure heart it causes blessings to come upon us. Ruth was in the right position to receive her husband and the Lord gave her conception. Her child was David's grandfather. Jesus Christ lineage traces back to the conception of Ruth's child. Because of her conception our Savior was born. Jesus Christ was the Son of David. Therefore, we are now privileged to have the gift of salvation.

{Ruth 4:11-17}

11 And all the people that were in the gate, and the elders, said, We are witnesses. The LORD make the woman that is come into thine house like Rachel and like Leah, which two did build the house of Israel: and do thou worthily in Ephratah, and be famous in Bethlehem:

12 And let thy house be like the house of Pharez, whom Tamar bare unto Judah, of the seed which the LORD shall give thee of this young woman.

13 So Boaz took Ruth, and she was his wife: and when he went in unto her, the Lord gave her conception, and she bare a son.

14 And the women said unto Naomi, Blessed be the LORD, which hath not left thee this day without a kinsman, that his name may be famous in Israel.

15 And he shall be unto thee a restorer of thy life, and a nourisher of thine old age: for thy daughter in law, which loveth thee, which is better to thee than seven sons, hath born him.

16 And Naomi took the child, and laid it in her bosom, and became nurse unto it.

17 And the women her neighbors gave it a name, saying, there is a son born to Naomi; and they called his name Obed: he is the father of Jesse, the father of David.

Testimonial

Dear Mama J,

I was reading my Bible before bed, this particular night I was reading Luke chapter twenty-three. As I was studying verse 27 jumped out at me. It stated, "And they followed him a great company of people and of women which also bewailed and lamented him." Earlier in this chapter they falsely accused Christ and sentenced him to death (crucifixion). As I read this I was like Whoa! Now I will continue to verse 28; but Jesus turning unto them and said, "Daughters of Jerusalem weep not for me but weep for yourself and your children." Verse 29 for behold the days are coming in which they shall say blessed are the barren and the wombs that never bare and the paps which never give suck. Lord have mercy, we are living in that day and age. People today consider you blessed if you have no children and look at you like you are a mess if you have some or more than what society approves. They are putting blessings on what should be condemned and condemning that which is blessed.

Minister Tamiko Orr Henry

Wow, did you get that? What a revelation the Lord has given Minister Orr. Imagine these women crying and sobbing for Jesus. He stopped them like hold up...Don't cry for me. He said cry for yourself and your children. Jesus himself said a day would come when it will be said, blessed is the barren womb. Be advised, birth control makes the womb barren. Jesus warned that; they will say that, the pap (breast) that has not given suck is blessed. I cannot tell you how many people in church has looked at me like I had three heads for breastfeeding my children. Please saints, be careful not to call evil good and good evil. This message is not for the world but the Church of God.

EXCEPT THE LORD
BUILD THE HOUSE

I have a question! If it was a curse to consume your
children by mouth in the bible, what is it when you consume
something by mouth to prevent your children today?

Lady Jay

Except the Lord Build the House

Once upon a time, I assumed the only way to build a house was with brick and mortar. Many women dream of building a house. However, they are not willing to let the Lord build their house with offspring. Psalms chapter one twenty-seven says, except the Lord build the house, they labour in vain that build it: except the LORD keep the city, the watchman waketh but in vain. Ironically, most women labour to build their life, while simultaneously forbidding life. They want nice houses, cars, education and material things, but use contraceptives.

I submit today, it is all in vain. Let the Lord build the house my sisters. I repeat, let the Lord build the house. God did not intend for us to build our house, but to leave that to him. How many saints sing, "We're blessed in the city, we're blessed in the field. Recently, I began to wonder do people realize that those words came from the Bible. Those words were a promise to the people from God, if they hearkened diligently to the voice of the Lord.

Deuteronomy 28 King James Version (KJV)

1 And it shall come to pass, if thou shalt hearken diligently unto the voice of the LORD thy God, to observe and to do all his commandments which I command thee this day, that the LORD thy God will set thee on high above all nations of the earth:

2 And all these blessings shall come on thee, and overtake thee, if thou shalt hearken unto the voice of the LORD thy God.

3 Blessed shalt thou be in the city, and blessed shalt thou be in the field.

Those words did not stand alone, not only was there a promise to be blessed in the city and the field. Blessed shall be the fruit of thy body the Bible speaks candidly.

{Deuteronomy 28:4}

4 Blessed shall be the fruit of thy body, and the fruit of thy ground, and the fruit of thy cattle, the increase of thy kine, and the flocks of thy sheep.

Deuteronomy chapter 28 spells out many blessings from the Lord as well as many curses. The Bible declares it shall come to pass, if you will not listen, all these curses will come upon thee. I was surprised to see recorded in scripture Curse shall be the fruit of thy body. Hopefully, we can all agree that when the Bible speaks of the fruit of the body, it is referring to offspring. I would like to go on record saying: "The basis of being a saint is having high regard for how God feels, and for what is recorded in the Bible. It is apparent in these verses that God feels that having children or offspring is a blessing. It is also apparent that not having them, it goes without saying. In other words, it is obvious!

The growing prosperity doctrine is plaguing the Body of Christ. How can anyone preach that gain is godliness, and not include being fruitful and multiplying?

Their ministries emphasize all scriptures that magnify abundance. However, they ignore abundance as it relates to the fruit of the womb. Some preach sow a seed to meet the need. Unfortunately, the seed of the body is not in that equation. Always remember that Godliness with contentment is great gain. Furthermore, contentment is a wonderful attribute. It has aided in my willingness to be fruitful and to multiply.

{I Timothy 6:3-8}

3 If any man teach otherwise, and consent not to wholesome words, even the words of our Lord Jesus Christ, and to the doctrine which is according to godliness;

4 He is proud, knowing nothing, but doting about questions and strifes of words,whereof cometh envy, strife, railings, evil surmisings,

5 Perverse disputings of men of corrupt minds, and destitute of the truth, supposing that gain is godliness: from such withdraw thyself.

6 But godliness with contentment is great gain.

7 For we brought nothing into this world, and it is certain we can carry nothing out.

8 And having food and raiment let us be therewith content.

A Godly Seed

Speaking of the Lord building our house made me think about marriage and how sacred it is. Malachi speaks on how God hates putting away, which is divorce. It encourages us to remember that a wife is her husband's companion. He encouraged men not to deal treacherously with the wife of his covenant. The chapter explains that God made man and woman one, that He (God) may seek a godly seed. Wow am I the only one that found it amazing to imagine God seeking for our seed. The seed or children that he expects us to train and teach to love him. Will he find our seed/children? Have we put of things for tomorrow, that was ordained for today? Have we put them on hold?

{Malachi 2:14-16}

Elders of old Versus Elders of Today

Ruth 4:8-14

8 Therefore the kinsman said unto Boaz, Buy it for thee. So he drew off his shoe.

9 And Boaz said unto the elders, and unto all the people, Ye are witnesses this day, that I have bought all that was Elimelech's, and all that was Chilion's and Mahlon's, of the hand of Naomi.

10 Moreover Ruth the Moabitess, the wife of Mahlon, have I purchased to be my wife, to raise up the name of the dead upon his inheritance, that the name of the dead be not cut off from among his brethren, and from the gate of his place: ye are witnesses this day.

11 And all the people that were in the gate, and the elders, said, we are witnesses. The Lord make the woman that is come into thine house like Rachel

and like Leah, which two did build the house of Israel: and do thou worthily in Ephratah, and be famous in Bethlehem:

12 And let thy house be like the house of Pharez, whom Tamar bare unto Judah, of the seed which the Lord shall give thee of this young woman.

I love this scenario. Boaz wanted to give honor to Ruth first husband, who had died, by keeping his name going. He looked forward to his wife conceiving a child(ren) in honor of her deceased husband. The people in the gate, and the elder's response too Boaz was so refreshing to me. It let me see how far society and even the church has fallen. The elders told Boaz, may the woman that come into thine house be like Rachel and like Leah. The two of them built the house of Israel. This passage is not referring to building a house with a hammer and nails. It is pointing out that Rachel and Leah had no reservations about having children.

The children of Israel that we read about today would not exist, if Rachel and Leah had many of today's women mentality about conceptions and childbirth. My husband spoke precisely saying, "The Elders at the gate endorsed the marriage, and fruitfulness of Boaz and Ruth's union. However, today many Elders would curse the fruitfulness of such a union. They despise the blessings of God as it relates to being fruitful and multiplying. For example, some would say phrases such as," I hope you are not pregnant again or Are you pregnant again?" Unfortunately, they are questioning one of God's original blessings bestowed upon mankind, which is to be fruitful and multiply." What my husband said is so profound. Many feel that they are doing you and God a service by praying that you will not conceive.

13 So Boaz took Ruth, and she was his wife: and when he went in unto her, the Lord gave her conception, and she bare a son.

14 And the women said unto Naomi, blessed be the Lord, which hath not left thee this day without a kinsman, that his name may be famous in Israel.

Boaz went in unto his wife and the Lord gave her conception. The Lord is the only one that can give conception. Contrary to popular belief, even when children are planted artificially without the Lord it would not be possible. I know this is true.

It happened to my high school bestie. She tried to conceive for three years, with three different doctors. She took four days of abdominal injections after her menstrual each month. Let's not forget the injections she took to make her release eggs. After many failed attempts and a financial burden, she conceived naturally after stopping the treatments. Remember we talked about the blessings and curses in Deuteronomy chapter twenty-eight.

Recorded in the fifty-third verse is one of the curses which says, "And thou shalt eat the fruit of thine own body, the flesh of thy sons and of thy daughters, which the Lord thy God hath given thee, in the siege, and in the straitness, wherewith thine enemies shall distress thee.

Please notice that it says, thou shalt eat the fruit of thine own body. It further explains, that he is referring to our sons and daughters that the Lord hath given. Here is the undeniable truth, the Lord has given many women sons and daughters, but through ingestion of contraceptives the children have become null and void. I have a question! If it was a curse to consume your children by mouth in the bible, what is it when you consume something by mouth to prevent your children today? The last part of that verse says, thine enemies shall distress thee. Can we not see that the enemy is distressing the world with blindness, so we cannot see that the fruit of the womb is God's reward to us?

Find in the verses below one of the first records of cannibalism, which is the practice of eating the flesh of one's own species.

II Kings 6:26-30

26 And as the king of Israel was passing by upon the wall, there cried a woman unto him, saying, Help, my lord, O king.

27 And he said, If the Lord do not help thee, whence shall I help thee? out of the barnfloor, or out of the winepress?

28 And the king said unto her, What aileth thee? And she answered, This woman said unto me, Give thy son, that we may eat him to day, and we will eat my son to morrow.

29 So we boiled my son, and did eat him: and I said unto her on the next day, Give thy son, that we may eat him: and she hath hid her son.

30And it came to pass, when the king heard the words of the woman, that he rent his clothes; and he passed by upon the wall, and the people looked, and, behold, he had sackcloth within upon his flesh.

The woman cried out in distress to the King. Another woman told her we will eat your son today, and my son tomorrow. Well, tomorrow came and the woman hid her child. She changed her mind, she did not want to consume her child after all. Meanwhile, the king was so grieved by the news that he rent his clothes. If a king in the Bible was grieved and found fault in a woman consuming a child with her mouth, how does the King of kings feel about women consuming birth control by mouth to prevent a child today? I can imagine the women felt their circumstances were so severe that the child should be sacrificed. It is similar with the purpose of birth control use today. Women feel their circumstances and livelihood calls for them to sacrifice their future children.

My husband put it like this, "During this time the country was under siege by their enemies, which led to severe famine. The famine led to cannibalism. Cannibalism was the byproduct and fulfilling of the prophecy recorded in Deuteronomy chapter 28. Today the average woman believe that times are so difficult that she must sacrifice her future children."

I will conclude this section with another question. What is the difference between a woman who ate her child, and a woman who ate birth control which by defaults get rid of a child.

Other Examples of Cannibalism in the Bible

Jeremiah 19:9   Deuteronomy 28:55-57
Lamentations 2:20   Ezekiel 5:10
Lamentation 4:10

I told you how tragic my miscarriage was. It took me a while to get over losing the baby. At times I blamed myself, I was on a strict exercise routine before I realized I was pregnant. The twins were almost four and growing like weeds. Nahum was diagnosed with Autism at age three. Having a special needs child helped me look at life a little different. Most of the things that are difficult for a special needs person, we take for granted daily. I love Nahum he is perfect, just perfect.

He helps me in more ways than one. He is considered nonverbal, but he has a big heart and a sweet spirit. I found myself saying, I want him to be my baby boy forever. I know God decides the gender of our children. However, I was excited when I learned I was pregnant again with another girl. Yes, friends' number ten! Wow, I am pregnant again! Yes, Nahum is still my baby boy! The pregnancy was stressful. High blood pressure and gestational diabetes landed me on bedrest most of the pregnancy. It was tolerable until another prenatal nightmare occurred. My blood pressure was so high, my doctor sent me to the hospital to stay for the remainder of my pregnancy. In hindsight it was like the scenario with the twins.

Unfortunately, there was an emotional rollercoaster that came with being in the hospital for six weeks. I had two Physicians overseeing my pregnancy, my primary and the High-Risk doctor. At this point, my primary doctor was done with my case since my health escalated to hospitalization. My High-Risk doctor and his team immediately started to stress the importance of having a C-section. After a couple weeks of me still not seeing things his way, he even sent my primary to try and convince me. He knew I loved and respected her. They said it was too risky, because I had four previous C-Sections.

I truly understood the risk of trying to delivery vaginally, but it still grieved me to think otherwise. I could only think, but what if I conceive again. The entire time I felt so grieved. My insides were telling me that a C-Section was going to be dreadful. I cried a lot, even the morning of. I woke up that morning so upset and fretful. I must admit I expected the epidural to be awful, and it was. It felt horrible the man kept jabbing me in my back.

When he finally finished it felt like before, so uncomfortable and abnormal. At this point tears are streaming down my face. I may have said this before, but it was as if a faucet was in my head because the tears was non-stop. To make a very long story short sobbing I began to tell my husband something is wrong with me. I don't know why I said that, but I kept repeating it. My husband eventually said, "Hey doc is everything ok?"

The response from the physician assisting my doctor nearly floored me. Why my doctor did not respond is beyond me, nevertheless, the physician said, "Yeah we just nicked her bowels." Wow, I was injured everything I thought and even worse was now upon me. I could not believe my doctor was not the one who answered. Furthermore, when were they going to inform me that six whole inches of my intestines had to be removed. I mean if you are going to have a bowel re-section should you not be informed in a respectable manner. The doctor continued saying to my husband, "You need to get fix, you got to stop having all these children."

He continued with slanderous verbiage. He considered our willingness to have children reckless. Our beautiful baby girl was a wonderful break from the thoughts bombarding me. She was seven pounds four ounces. I had to shake the fact that all the staff surrounding me in the C-section was aware of the mishap with my intestines. What ever happen to saying, "Mrs. Jones we cut your bowels by mistake, we are going to get a surgeon right away." No, they had contacted the surgeon and did not let us know until we asked.

Meanwhile, in recovery I was loopy, but I do recall a sweet spirited doctor introducing himself to me. He told me I did your bowel re-section, I'm here if you need me. Well, not only did I need him, I needed the Lord desperately. As the night progressed I became ill. I started projectile vomiting. I said to my husband, "I believe I have pneumonia."

Later I developed a fever, that is when they sent me to another floor to be monitored closely. I continued to projectile vomit several days, I experienced some dark hours. It was confirmed that I aspirated and had pneumonia. That sweet doctor was a man of his words, even though I was nearly lifeless I recall seeing his face daily checking on me. I can still see in my mind his concerned facial expression. He left a lasting impression on me one day he could not make it, he sent someone. He even had the nurse call me to let me know he was checking on me.

My situation was looking bleak for a minute. I learned that I developed an ileus and it took days for my bowels to wake up after the surgery. I did not see baby Phebe for a few days because I was just so ill. One sweet nurse realized how long it had been. She went and got Phebe and tucked her in my gown, so I could spend time with her. I was too weak to hold her. There is no way I could describe this story play for play, But I thank God for bringing me out. I remember Juicy came to see me one day she was letting YouTube play, this was typical for her. I don't' remember much of that day, but a song came on that literally revived me. The words said concerning Jesus, Death could not hold you down. Tears began to flow from my eyes. I knew that day that I was at death's door, I also realized death was not going to hold me down. #Juicy

Believe it or not my doctor never came back to do rounds on me. I just could not believe after nearly causing my death he never came back to check on me. Unfortunately, Mr. you need to get fix came by one day. He decided to take advantage of the fact that I was alone. He stood flat footed in my hospital room, and said, "You need to figure out how you going to stop having all these babies. He said, the next time it's going to be worse."

I think I pretty much went blank after a few more statements like the before mentioned. I did report him and my doctor to the hospital administration. In summary, I yet thank God for my child. I have many regrets about the physical and emotional pain that surrounded Phebe's birth, but she is not one of them. We truly thank God for Phebe Abigail, as my Sister Pernita would call her.

The sweet doctor that repaired my bowels was so ecstatic at my follow-up appointment. He told me that we had the same birthdate and born in the same year. My, my, my, that touched me so strongly. His wife had just delivered a baby also. I told him that we are twin friends from here out. God had him handpicked to save my life. I later learned that my high-risk doctor who cut my intestines stopped practicing in my city. He moved away. Right, seems suspect!

JESUS IS A MIRACLE
WORKER

The condition is called Peripartum Cardiomyopathy. She said, "I know you don't want to hear this, but we ask moms to terminate the pregnancy in these cases

Lady Jay

Jesus is a Miracle Worker

As you can see trouble seems to find me when it is time to deliver my babies. Many feels, that is a sign that I should have stopped a long time ago. I feel I have a record-breaking survival rate, therefore it is proof that they all were predestined. Before they were formed in the belly God knew them. My nephew passed away about seven months after Phebe was born. Shortly after that, my dad became ill. He passed away three months after my nephew.

I eventually hired a personal trainer, it was finally time to get rid of my baby fat. My husband would take me to my classes. They were tough. I prayed so much trying to do those exercises, one girl said she about to tarry for the Holy Ghost. That was so funny, but thankfully I already had the Holy Ghost. Coming home from class one night my husband says, "Baby I know you enjoying your classes… but I think you should make sure you are not pregnant first." I was like, are you serious? I bought my cute tennis shoes, my exercise shirt, with the slot for my thumb! I weighed in and started my goal. We picked up a test that night. The test was positive, it had a faint line. That was not enough for me, I took two more test. Both tests were positive.

I did not stop there I took two more test, yes, a total of five test. How does this guy know this stuff? He always seems to have the revelation that I am with child before I do. Goodbye exercise, I stay no longer with you. Not that you cannot exercise while pregnant. I had bigger fish to fry. Instantly, my heart was filled with concern about the last C-section and the bowel re-section. I must admit I was so shocked about being pregnant I had to confirm once more. I walked in to a local resource center to be tested. They did an ultrasound as well. I was told that the gestational sac was empty. She said to follow up with my doctor, it could be too early. I followed up with my doctor, took another ultrasound which also revealed an empty sac. Meanwhile, I was having severe shortness of breath. My doctor ordered a heart examine, she feared I had a condition that causes women to have a heart attack while pregnant. The condition is called Peripartum Cardiomyopathy. She said, "I know you don't want to hear this, but we ask moms to terminate the pregnancy in these cases.

I was terrified, my friend Nikki left her job. Honey, I don't know who cried the most, her or me! Thank God the heart test came out fine. By now it's time to take another ultrasound, which revealed yes, another empty sac. They did blood levels, that all returned low, signs of a failed pregnancy. I was diagnosed with a blighted ovum. That means the sperm and egg came together but the child did not form. I was scheduled for a D&C to remove the empty sac from my body.

Oh, my goodness, I was once again terrified. Prophetess Collins and I was on the phone one day having us a sad friend boo hoo session. She suddenly began to pray and prophesy, that it will be for God's Glory. She let the Lord have his way. The doctor said the day before the D&C, "I want to check one more time. I want to wait one week to do it." I came back one week later, lo and behold a twelve-week-old baby pops up on the screen! No Kidding! I was so blown away, but I was not the only one. My doctor came in with her arms stretched out saying, "Girl what the heck?" Her hairs were standing straight up on her arms. You could see the chill bumps. I said, you know who did that! (Jesus)

We rejoiced, and I was off to a great start. Only God can spare a child in the womb from death. What made this story amazing is remember when I had the miscarriage, the doctor asked me to put the D&C off for one week. Following those orders nearly killed me, Remember I bled out. God had my mind blank to protect her. If I had remembered what happen I would have said, "oh no, I will not wait one week for the D&C." Fear from my previous experience would have caused me to make a rash decision.

Ironically, I was twelve weeks when I miscarried, and I was twelve weeks when baby Miracle was discovered by ultrasound. What an amazing discovery! Speaking of fear, I changed doctors. I was afraid of falling into the hands of the staff that assisted my High-Risk doctor. I love my new doctor he was a Christian He had Scriptures throughout his office. My pregnancy went pretty good for the most part, until I fell at eight months.

Yes, I fell and dislocated my shoulder. Let me tell you, that was the worse pain ever! I had to have help from head to toe. Two weeks later I started contracting on a Friday. Pastor, Sister Nikki and I went out to eat that night the contractions continued the entire time.

By time I settled down for bed they stopped. Well they picked back up later in the night, then my water broke. I was so excited, but my husband felt at day break we should head to the hospital. When we arrived everything was rush rush rush. I was in labor, my pressure was up, and it was my doctor weekend off. The on call doctor explained to me, that she was uncomfortable doing my surgery alone. Only God knows what was on my records that made her feel that way. She said she was going to call my doctor and ask him to come.

Thank God he did come. Thank God again, it was not like the previous doctor said, worse. His words, "Next time will be worse did not come to pass. It was amazing, the best C-Section out of my now six surgeries. I cannot explain it but it felt like I had a vaginal birth. My pressure did continue to rise to dangerous levels. They had to give me several medications and it took a few days to come down. One of my nurses said to me, "I was so concerned for you last night I called to check on you." She said, I said a prayer for you." It was just a blessing to have such sweetness surrounding me while I was in a crisis. God stepped in and everything got better in the process of time. I am thankful for all my children. I have endured a lot of suffering bringing them into the world. Nevertheless, I would not trade any of them. I consider it a privilege to partner with my husband being parents.

I ask that you pray about this topic earnestly. Medical interventions are good in their places, but "if it ain't broke don't try to fix it." Be sure to make a righteous judgment call concerning conception and childbirth His way. Remember God is seeking for a godly seed, can he depend on you. Parenting is not easy, but it is one hundred percent worth it. Women of God should have joy about baring children.

The kind of Joy that Hannah had. Make no mistake, in his presence is the fullness of Joy. Therefore, I have concluded that a woman truly living in the presence of the Lord, can receive the words recorded in this book with gladness. I will explain it in a quote I once heard, "Truth and error are not on equal standards." "Usually the wrong answers outnumber the right answers."

"One right answer can be mixed in with billions of wrong answers." So, I conclude, compelling you saying it behooves us to take heed to ourselves and the doctrine or teaching that we embrace. Furthermore, elder women please be teachers of GOOD THINGS. The world is not teaching us how to love our husband and our children. The world is not teaching us biblical standards. Lastly, I feel blessed to behold Delvin, Barry, Zachery, Hannah, Marion, Temperance, Nathan, Nahum, and Naomi Phebe and Miracle face-to-face. I remember the pain of each experience no more; except to praise my God for keeping me. My fellow sisters you can do all things through Christ who strengthens you. Be encouraged to have conception and childbirth His (Christ) way.

I have certainly learned the hard way, going against the grain can affect your life for years. Do you remember the young girl who had the abortion, but received redemption and forgiveness after watching a spiritual play? That young girl was me.

Rest in peace my two angels
Conception and childbirth his (Christ) way

Thank you

FAMILY

Mom & Boys

Mom & Girls

Mom & Guys

Mom & Girls

Miracle

Phebe

The Holy land Experience

Last Day in Condo 2017

The top picture is what they saw on three different Ultrasounds while pregnant with Miracle, which was an empty sac. The bottom picture is 12-week-old baby which is what was discovered after waiting one week.

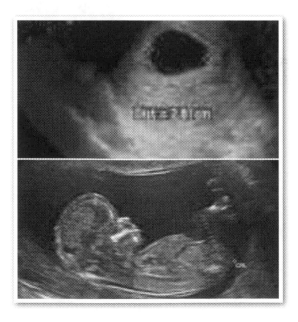

"We thank God for Miracle I call her Chunk-a-Wunk"

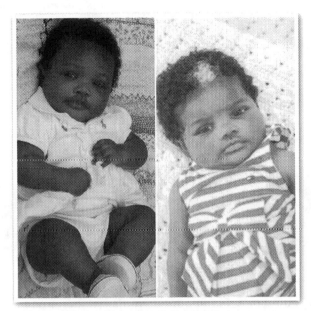

Phebe Abigail & Miracle Unique

Barry & LaShela Jones

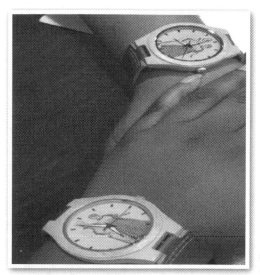

"Time is of Essence, Be fruitful and multiply"

In this picture I was pregnant with the child I lost in February of 2014. Ladies take pictures of yourself during your pregnancy. You get each pregnancy once. Thank God I have this picture as a memorial of my sweet baby that passed away.

Pastor Barry Delloyd Jones Sr.

Happy Is the Man that hath his quiver full of them: they shall not be ashamed, but they shall speak with the enemies in the gate Psalm 127:5

FINAL COMMENTS FROM THE AUTHOR

Perhaps your heart has been touched by reading this book. Please know that this book was not intended to bring condemnation, but to educate and reconcile the hearts of women back to God's word. If your heart has been pricked this is the perfect time to repent and ask God for his forgiveness. He is near those who are of a broken heart and a contrite Spirit. Please be blessed by the following information.

Elect-Lady LaShela Jones

From the Desk of Pastor Barry Jones ...

Praise the Lord, if you are not born again, the following will be the proper steps to take. Believe by faith that Jesus is the Messiah and savior of the world, and that he died and rose again from the grave. 2.

Ask Jesus to forgive you of all sins that you have committed. The Bible says that all have sinned and come short of the glory of God. (Romans 3:23) Yes, all of us have sinned. Therefore, repent! This means to change your lifestyle, ways, purpose, and thinking to match your new life. When you repent, you let sin go or turn away from all activity associated with sinful behavior. All should be baptized in water, in the name of Jesus Christ for the remission of sins. Ask Jesus to fill you with the gift of the Holy Ghost with the evidence of speaking in tongues or other languages. The tongues are a heavenly inspired untaught language. Continue in the teachings of the apostles as recorded in the epistles of the New Testament.

The word of God clearly teaches that some believers received the Holy Spirit prior to water baptism. Therefore, the sequence may vary. Please don't forget that each day brings us closer to death and judgment. Today is your day for True Salvation in Jesus Christ. If God is pricking your heart today, find a Church that teaches and preaches what Jesus Christ and the Apostles taught regarding salvation as recorded in Mark 16:15-18. John 3:1-8 and Acts chapters 2, 8, 10, 19.

Also learn and do the teachings of Jesus Christ as recorded in the Gospels of Matthew, Mark, Luke and John. Read both the Old and New Testament.

Be a doer of the word of God for the rest of your lives depart from evil and do good. Always remember that true repentance is turning away from sin and changing your life style and mind toward those things which are pleasing to Jesus Christ according to the bible. Please don't forget that as new believers we should cleanse ourselves from all filthiness of the flesh and spirit perfecting holiness in the fear of God. (11Cor 7:1) Always remember that Jesus loves you and if you love him you will keep his commandments. (John14:15)

Pastor Barry Jones Sr.

Please purchase your Copy of the books:

True Salvation in Jesus Christ: By Pastor Barry Jones Sr.

Ye Shall Be as God: By LaShela Jones

Get a Copy of our CD: **It's Time to Praise the Lord**

You can contact us personally or find Pastor Barry Jones Sr. & Elect-Lady Jones music on:

Reverbnation: ITunes
Hmv Digital CD Baby Amazon.com CD Universe
Facebook: Pas Sta Jones
Twitter: @hiselect1
Email: electladyljones@yahoo.com
Email: Conception4Him@gmail.com